EMPATH SURVIVAL GUIDE AND NARCISSISTIC RELATIONSHIP

2-in-1 Book

Learn How to Protect Yourself From Narcissists, Toxic Relationships and Emotional Abuse + Recovery Plan & 30 Day Challenge

EMPATH
THE SURVIVAL GUIDE FOR HIGHLY SENSITIVE PEOPLE

Protect Yourself From Narcissists & Toxic Relationships. Discover How To Stop Absorbing Other People's Pain

Table of Contents

Introduction..7

Chapter One - Are You an Empath?...............................10
    What is an Empath?..10
    10 Signs You're An Empath..11
    Empathic, Introverted and Sensitive: What is the Difference?....14
    8 Misconceptions About Empaths 16

Chapter Two - Understanding the Empath Gift..........19
    The Science Behind Empathy and Empaths 20

Chapter Three - The Empath Reality 33
    5 Bad Habits that Empaths Must Let Go............................35
    The 5 Common Health Problems of Empaths 36

Chapter Four - The Injured Empath..............................40
    What is Compassion Fatigue?..42
    Signs of an Injured Empath 45
    Beware: The Victim Complex...47
    The Truth About Empaths and Addiction............................49

Chapter Five - The Dangers of Being an Empath........52
    Why Narcissists Are Drawn to Empaths.............................55
    Why Empaths are Drawn to Narcissists 56
    Signs an Empath is with an Emotional Vampire................57

Chapter Six - Healing the Empath Heart 62
    5 Healing Activities for Empaths to Relax 62
    Powerful Techniques for Healing and Self-Protection.................67
    Positive Affirmations All Empaths Must Know 69

Chapter Seven - The Healthy, Happy Empath 71
    The 5 Powerful Lessons Every Empath Must Learn 71
    Daily Practices of a Healthy Empath....................................73
    Stop Empathizing with Pain and Start Empathizing with Joy 76

Chapter Eight - Empathy as a Superpower 79

The 7 Natural Gifts that All Empaths Possess 79
The Best Jobs for Empaths 81
Conclusion 87

Empath Survival Guide

Introduction

There is a unique breed of individuals who are gifted with the ability to not only experience their emotions and those of the people around them; they can also experience the physical pain of other people. These individuals walk into a room and within minutes, they can accurately pick on the vibes of the people in the room. This may sound like a cool superpower that belongs on the set of X-Men but in reality, it is something that can be very difficult to deal with and not many people are emotionally and mentally equipped to manage these gifts. You may identify such persons as people who are overly sensitive. Psychology experts profile them as empaths and their story is not always one of those happily ever after types.

For the longest time, emotions have been frowned on as a weakness and displaying them was described as a feminine trait at best. In worst-case scenarios, people who showed their emotions one too many times were regarded as persons who have no control over how they feel. Derogatory terms like "unpredictable", "walking eggshells", "cry baby" and so many other names that are not fit to print are used to tag people who dare to show their emotions. The general negative perception about emotions has woven itself into the very foundation of the society which is the family. There are a lot of families today who enforce strict measures to deter any display of emotions at home. This need to shut down a very crucial aspect of one's self has led many to suffer silently for a better part of their lives. For an empath, they live with the double trauma of dealing with their own emotions as well as the pain of others. This leaves them constantly emotionally overwhelmed. If you picked up this book, chances are you are an empath or you know an empath who struggles with their emotional burden.

But, what if I told you that those very emotions that you feel cripple you and your ability to thrive can be channeled into making you a better version of yourself and in so doing, you can enrich your life? Sounds too good to be true right? Well, here is one truth that many of us heard but don't really believe because they have been dumped in the same category as those ineffective life clichés people dish out. Your emotions are anything but weak. In fact, it is described as one of the most powerful forces possessed by humans and before we go any further in this book, I can tell you that shutting your emotions down is not going to do you any good. The only way forward is to embrace those feelings by choosing to accept your abilities as an empath.

Being an empath goes beyond understanding your emotions. As an empath, you embrace the emotions of others. The wealth of understanding you acquire in this process gifts you with a unique perspective of the world and the people that you encounter daily. This goes a long way to help you foster relationships that are more meaningful and impactful. Most importantly, as an empath, you develop a deeper connection with yourself that truly empowers you to understand pain. This is not some new-age psychobabble fad that is trending at the moment. This is you taking back the power from people who have tagged the way you truly feel as weak and evolving into the "real you" that you are meant to be.

With this book, you can finally take off the mask you have been forced to wear by the society and step into your reality. As an empath who had to navigate the process of my "becoming" without a guide, I know how difficult to make sense of how you feel. I spent lots of hours daily scouring through the internet for information on these rainbows of emotions that I go through every day. I have come close to several breakdowns not because I had a lot of bad experiences or that I was taking on more workload than I normally would. I was just constantly overwhelmed by what I was feeling. People would come to me with their problems because I had a knack for being such a great listener and I could connect with them in ways that they found comforting. However, I also ended up having to deal with the emotional aftermath of their predicaments. I sought counseling and for a while, that helped me. But, I still sought validation from the people I deal with on a day to day basis. I didn't want to crumble emotionally in front of them so that I could keep being their go-to counselor.

This meant I had to act like I had my life together 100% of the time even if in reality, it felt like I could barely keep the seams from falling apart. In very succinct terms, I was a mess. With the contents of this book, I was able to;

- Make sense of the emotions I was feeling
- Find the strength to embrace these seemingly chaotic parts of myself
- Learn to manage my emotions better
- Unlock my natural intuitive nature and pay more attention to my instincts
- Become better at managing my relationships with people

Maybe you are reading my story and feeling like you are looking into the mirror of your own life. Here is an assurance, if I can find my way back, so can you. However, there is a caveat. Living as an empath requires you being deliberate about your decisions. Anything less could send you on a downward spiral to a dark place that not many people recover from. Before you flip over to the next chapter, I want you to take a moment and decide right here, right now that you are going to be more deliberate about the choices that you make going forward.

That said, the information you would receive in this book are practical steps you can take daily to help you better manage your emotions while navigating the murky emotional waters of other people. At the end of this book, you should be able to stand on a rooftop and proudly declare that you know who you are. That knowledge is powerful and very uplifting. So, to begin the next chapter of your life, turn over to the next page. Things are about to get exciting.

Empath Survival Guide

Chapter One - Are You an Empath?

I was a teenager when I had my first encounter with the word "empath." It was from a television series that was popular at the time. In this series, the empath was portrayed as someone who was gifted with divine powers and the ability to feel everything the people around them felt. This empath could feel their pain, their joy, their anger, and even their fears. In this fictional world, the powers of the empath were transferable but if anyone other than a true empath attempted to take these powers, they would be crushed by the weight of the emotions they were forced to experience. This interpretation of an empath is certainly fascinating but it is also very extreme.

Sci-fi lovers share a similar view with the creators of this fantasy series. Culturally, empaths are believed to be humans who possess this paranormal ability to accurately sense the emotional state of others. A popular empath in today's sci-fi trend would be Mantis from the movie, *Guardians of the Galaxy*. Again, this is all very cool but reality tells us a different story.

What is an Empath?

An empath is simply a person with a heightened awareness of the emotions around them. Beyond this awareness, empaths tend to show a lot of empathy towards other people – so much they can experience the emotions of others as if they were their own. Empaths don't just observe people; they have the innate ability to experience them from the inside. The term "ability" is used loosely here. It does not connote the existence of supernatural traits, rather it is directed at a personality trait that uniquely defines them.

In psychology, empaths are described as people who have a great amount of empathy for others. Given everything I've explained so far, it might feel a little disappointing to see empaths defined with such simplicity. Empaths are powerfully unique because they can sense emotions that the people around them try to hide. Without the right information, however, this "uniqueness" can cause a lot of frustration. That said, how can you tell if you are truly an empath and not simply projecting what you hope you are?

I have compiled a list that explores the characteristics of most empaths. If you relate to six or more of the following traits, you are likely an empath.

10 Signs You're An Empath

1. Crowded spaces cause you to feel overwhelmed

When you are in a sea of people, their emotions wash over you like waves and for a person who has a tendency to feel everything, it can leave you feeling overwhelmed. The sensation is akin to experiencing sensory overload where all of your senses are firing off in different directions.

2. You personalize the experiences of others

When a friend comes to you with stories that have strong emotional content, you don't just listen and try to gauge their current state of mind. You see yourself walking in their shoes and reliving their experiences as if they happened to you. At the end of that conversation, you are not just an observer but an active participator in the event. This leaves you just as emotionally riled up as the person who shared their experience with you.

3. You are labeled as "emotional" or "too sensitive"

The way people describe you can give a little insight into your personality. Again, it is not often accurate but it speaks to the actions carried out by you that lead to the general perception of you as any being either too emotional or too sensitive. Now being emotional goes beyond the ability to cry at the drop of the hat. It infers that you get riled up easily.

4. Dealing with people leaves you feeling exhausted

There are people who go through an entire rainbow of emotions in a matter of minutes and these kinds of people can be exhausting to deal with even for the regular person. For an empath, it is twice as bad. You might speak with the mildest mannered person and still get exhausted. Why? Because you can sense the genuine emotions underneath the polite façade. Empaths have a strong radar for someone's true feelings, and they are rarely fooled by pretenses.

5. Most people feel understood by you

This one is a no brainer because you actually understand people. Your ability to see things from their perspective and empathize with them gives you a unique connection to them. In a weird but commendable way, you have this "you are them" bond that puts you in their shoes. For this reason, people tend to be drawn to you. They may feel seen in ways they don't normally feel seen. Sadly, not many people understand empaths, except for other empaths.

6. You are mostly an introvert

Your need to deal with people in very limited doses puts you on the outside of social events, but you likely don't mind it that much. You may even take pleasure in it. Empaths are more likely to be introverted because absorbing the emotions of others can get exhausting, so they tend to need a lot of alone time. Extroverted empaths do exist, but they are rare.

7. You can intuitively sense emotions

This is a big indicator that you are an empath. You are hardly ever fooled by the exterior charms and smiling façade. And if a person makes the mistake of coming to you with lies, you can detect it in a heartbeat without even having to ask questions. There is no technique to this when it comes to you. You are not looking out for that elevated pulse, dilated pupils, or sweaty palms. An empath just knows.

8. You feel connected to nature

This is another general human trait. It is not definitive but it is very common with empaths. Your connection to nature goes beyond the love of trees and sounds of chirping birds. These things give you pleasure but they also give you a sense of rejuvenation. Some people feel replenished after a good night's rest, some seek solace in food but for you, nature is what gets your juices up and flowing.

9. You can never say no to a person in need

Your experiences of other people's pain, suffering or joy does not end with you "feeling" what they feel. It compels you to act. You are not going to leave that little girl crying in the corner simply because her mom is there with her. You want to help make her feel better. Dropping a few coins in the cup for that homeless man is not going to cut it for you. You go home, grab a nice pair of socks, a warm and lovingly used blanket and hand it to him. And if that man stops coming to the area, you might be one of the first to notice. Because empaths have a hard time saying no, many of them struggle with taking on more than they can handle. They want to help everyone, and this can leave them feeling drained.

10. You can empathize with nearly everyone

It's not just about feeling the emotions of homeless people and crying children. Let's face it, it's easy to empathize with the vulnerable people in our society, and any kind person would. Empaths can feel empathy for basically everyone. If two people get in a fight, an empath may not agree with the actions of the aggressor, but they can still have empathy for them. They are able to pinpoint the feelings that caused the person to behave that way and they can empathize with that deep need. A true sign of an empath is when they can emotionally connect with someone that everyone else has turned away from.

Before you started this book, you likely already suspected you were an empath. Now that you've affirmed this, how does it feel? I remember how relieved I felt to finally discover the concept of an empath. It can be a liberating experience to finally identify with something, and to know you're not alone.

Now, let's clear up something important. There are a few words that are used interchangeably with the word "empath.' They may have been used to describe certain aspects of an empath but they do not in any way mean that a person who possesses these qualities is an empath. It is important to provide a clear distinction so as to avoid confusion going forward.

Empathic, Introverted and Sensitive: What is the Difference?

Let us start with the standard dictionary definition of these words before we explore it in depth. A person who is described as empathic essentially shows the ability to understand and share the feelings of another person. An introvert, on the other hand, is a shy and reclusive person who feels more energized when they spend time with themselves. And finally, a sensitive person is someone who is quick to react to the actions or reactions of others. As we can see, these are three different traits with three different meanings. While it is quite possible for a true empath to possess each of these three traits, none of these traits alone can make you an empath.

There are people who have the ability to empathize with others. They feel bad for the pain another person is going through but that does not make them all empaths. Empathy is a wonderful human trait that can give birth to kindness. Empaths, on the other hand, don't just feel bad about the pain of others, they personalize it and make it their own. It takes skillful discipline for an empath to get to a place where their interpretation of the pain of others does not cripple them emotionally.

Some empaths become introverted because they want to hide away from the distress that frequent interactions with people cause them. However, they need those interactions with people to fully make use of their empathic abilities. If they continue to hide away in solitude, that empathic nature may become buried and they'll simply become introverts. Now introverts actually derive pleasure in being alone. Beyond the basic necessity of human interaction (and even then, with very limited people), the introvert takes no pleasure in engaging with people outside of those they have a bond with. For empaths, this solitude is meant to provide a brief reprieve from the onslaught of emotions that hits them during social interactions.

Finally, being sensitive does not immediately translate to a hyper-awareness of the emotions of other people. In fact, in many cases, it can speak to a heightened awareness of only the self. Sensitive people can be acutely aware of their wants and needs, or at the very least, when they're not getting what they want and need. They have a fixed perception of what they feel is right or wrong and when words, actions or perceived reactions go against this information they have of themselves, they react. Even when they react to information affecting others, it is usually centered on their perception of the experiences of others. Many arrogant and narcissistic individuals can be accurately described as sensitive, and they are the opposite of an empath. Ever seen a narcissist get emotional because they aren't getting their way? Exactly. Many narcissists may even call themselves empaths as a way to excuse their inappropriate emotions, but never forget, a true empath must have empathy for other people.

In summary, these can be wonderful traits to have as a person and depending on your personality type, they can serve you well. However, there is more to being an empath than this. Generally speaking, the misuse of certain words to identify an empath are not the only misconceptions out there.

8 Misconceptions About Empaths

1. Empaths are weak

This is just one of the many derogatory labels used by people who do not understand the compassion of an empath. These people look down on any display of emotion other than anger. In reality, empaths can be some of the strongest people you'll ever meet. It can be exhausting to feel so many emotions so easily, and it takes true strength to rise again after feeling so overwhelmed.

2. Empaths cannot be leaders

An organization where there is no form of empathy in management would result in a toxic environment where workers cannot thrive, and they may eventually abandon their posts. An empathic leader is not constantly overflowing with emotions; an empathic leader can simply see his or her employees as human beings, and not just cogs in their machines. Leaders who can empathize with their employees will be more liked by those employees. And when workers in an organization have mutual respect for one another, that organization instantly becomes a fantastic team.

3. Empaths cannot be rational

I believe this is the biggest misconception of them all. An empath is someone who has more than just the facts when they conduct their analyses. Their ability to combine facts with the knowledge they draw from their emotional well gives them a more complete picture of the situation at hand. An empath is not bogged down by emotions in their decision-making, they simply have more information to act on. Empaths may take longer to make a decision, since they have more to consider, but empathy does not impede someone's sense of rationality.

4. Empaths are psychic

This is one of those myths that I wish we didn't have to dispel. Given the accuracy with which an empath can decipher true emotions and catch a liar mid-act, you have to wonder if there is some supernatural angle to it. There's nothing supernatural about it. Empaths are just very skilled at reading microexpressions, tone, and body language. They don't pick up these emotions out of nowhere, the signs are there all along; it's just that most people can't read them.

5. All empaths are introverts

The fact is, most empaths display some introverted tendencies but they are not always introverts. There are plenty of empaths who are extroverts, and many of them are better at hiding it when they feel emotionally overwhelmed. They still need time to recharge and reboot after social scenarios, but they feel more compelled to get back out there once they've had the rest they need.

6. Empaths are fictional characters made up by comic books

I want to launch into a litany of words to disprove this but the fact that you and I exist is enough to show this is not true. Psychologists have publicly acknowledged that empaths do exist and they can even identify what makes us the way we are. Do we need more evidence than that?

7. Empaths are always crying and over-emotional

Most people expect an empath to have an emotional meltdown every hour or so. Our abilities as empaths allow us to access a doorway that not many people can reach and sometimes, what we find on the other side can be very disconcerting and in some cases overwhelming. But, that image of the empath who is constantly in the fetal position crying their eyes out is completely inaccurate. While empaths *can* get very emotional, only a small percentage of empaths are in that state permanently. After a while, empaths learn to cope with their gift. They tend to be aware of when they need to withdraw to prevent themselves from getting to that state.

8. Empaths are victims of trauma

Many victims of trauma can turn out to be empaths, but it's never caused by the trauma itself. Sometimes empaths can live perfectly lucky and stable lives, without much exposure to trauma at all, and they'll still strongly empathize with those who are different from them. This is what makes empaths so incredible. Most people need to experience something to learn from it, but empaths can absorb it instantly.

Chapter Two - Understanding the Empath Gift

Given everything that you've felt in your lifetime, you may feel reluctant to regard empathic qualities or abilities as a gift. And who can blame you? Your emotional journey up to this point has been akin to a rollercoaster ride. Most people have difficulty processing the emotions that they encounter. An empath can go through a whole menu of emotions before the morning is over and that is not all. You experience these emotions at a level of intensity that would normally erode what I like to call your emotion nerve points (they are like the numbers on the scale except, in this case, they are not assessing your weight but your limits). Many people would be broken if they were to experience a fraction of what you feel. At this point, you and your emotions are like a mountain with an active volcano. Your exterior hides the turmoil going on inside.

You are probably thinking, "This part-time writer and full-time empath is doing a poor job of selling the idea of seeing your empathic abilities as a gift." Well, that's because everything I've outlined can indeed be considered a weakness, if looked at through the wrong lens. But do you want to know a secret? You can easily make this weakness your superpower. You just need to know how.

Your ability to process a variety of emotions faster than the average person takes a lot of strength. The way you experience emotions and interactions with so much depth is a new kind of intelligence. And to be the human equivalent of a volcano? Come on! How awesome is that?

Many people consider the empath gift as a superpower, but it can actually be explained with science. Let's get deeper, shall we?

The Science Behind Empathy and Empaths

The explanations I've given for empathy, until now, have come from a psychological and experiential point of view. But what does science have to say about it? A surprising amount of research has been done on the subject, and there are more than a handful of theories out there to explain the empath experience. Some of these theories are hogwash and would not hold their own in any science court. I found a few quite interesting.

I examined as many scientific theories as possible in the course of my research. I sorted them into different folders: the utterly crazy, the science-fiction and the ones that truly gave me pause. I'll share the best theories that made the most sense to me. And how about just one of the silly ones to end on a laugh?

Theory #1:

The guys who spend their careers studying the brain had to get a top spot on this list and they did not disappoint. According to them, empaths behave the way they do because of the mirror effect. The mirror effect essentially tells us that when we see someone do something, the part of our brains that is responsible for executing those same actions is triggered. Without our realization, that action is executed neurologically. And even though in reality, that action was never carried out by us, our brain relays the information to us as though we've truly performed those actions. Subsequently, we experience the consequences of those actions first-hand as if they happened to us.

Let's say your friend tells you about their horrible breakup and how she had to pack up all her ex-partner's things into a suitcase. An empathic person immediately puts themselves in that position. It's almost as if you were there yourself, packing away the belongings of the person you're about to say goodbye to forever. You weren't there, but it feels real to you. You feel the sadness in its entirety. The part of your brain that would be active during that scenario is, indeed, active now. And all you needed was to hear the story from your friend. That's the life of an empath.

I am willing to bet that you've experienced this before. According to neuroscientists, when we see a person take a certain action, our brain tells us we've done the same thing and we experience what they feel. Neurologically speaking, we have actually walked a mile in their shoes.

The focus of the study was on empathy and not empaths in particular. And what it proved is that empathy is a choice. Yes, you read that right. The brain's transmission of signals may have sounded like an involuntary reaction such as a blinking reflex, but actually, the brain decides in less than a nanosecond whether it's going to engage in the mirror effect. The display of empathy becomes a choice. Psychopaths adamantly refuse to participate in that process by deliberately detaching themselves emotionally.

This second study fine-tuned the purpose of their research. It was not just about empathy in this case now. It was meant to explain why some people are more empathetic than others. The person in charge of this project decided against using the word 'empath.' Instead, 'altruist' was used. It is important to note that there are different types of altruists. You have the kin-based altruist. As the name implies, these guys are very empathetic towards people they consider closely related to them. A mother who keenly experiences the anguish of her child displays empathy like no other but that does not really make her an empath now, does it? The second group of altruists is classified under the reciprocity-based group. They are what I like to call, the scratch my back and I scratch your back type of giver. For them, a favor is a bond that they hold in high esteem with every intention of paying it forward no matter the cost to them. You ever watch those movies where the hero calls on an 'old friend' who owes him a favor to help him or her complete a mission. More often than not, this old friend dies but not before telling the hero that they have paid their debt [so sad when that happens]. Well, that is what we are talking about here. And then you have the third group of guys who do what they do simply because they genuinely care about the welfare of the person that they are doing this good deed for. They do not have to have a prior relationship with the person and as a matter of fact, the people in this group prefer to do their generous giving anonymously. These non-cape wearing heroes are classified as care-based altruists in the experiment and they were the main focus in this research. That said, let us get back to the research.

The participants in this where people who had done selfless acts like donating an organ to a complete stranger and other really cool stuff [that might have you considering what your next 'giving' would be if you know what I mean]. They were paired with people who have never done that and both groups were asked to look at different images showing different emotional expressions. Their brains were mapped to monitor their reaction to these images and the results documented. What it showed was that the amygdalae which are the portion of the brain responsible for processing emotions among other things appeared to be 8 percent bigger than the regular non-altruist in the group which is incredible. Of course, they also examined the other guys at the other end [the psychopaths] and what they found was that the amygdalae of psychopaths were 18 percent smaller than average. Now, this made sense to me. The idea that empaths are essentially people with a neurological bonus in the right are. Who knew 8 percent could make that much of a difference, right? But this brain phenomenon was not the only thing that stood them apart. Other aspects of their lives were studied and it showed that they [the care-based altruists] were evidently more humble than their peers. This is why they reacted to the pain and fears of complete strangers as though it were their own. And this brings us to the point of this research. The research was guided by the role that fear plays in the decisions made by altruists. Let me break that down for you.

Empath Survival Guide

Empaths are more than just givers. The key thing for empaths is experiencing the emotions of others as though it were their own. There are no limits to the range of emotions that they feel. They can feel the rage of others, the pain, and even their joys. This experiment focused on the giving aspect of empathy and not just the experiential element which is crucial to the full definition of an empath. The researchers wanted to find out if there was a way to clearly identify true empaths. I would say that what this was able to successfully achieve was tell us that some people are visibly more sensitive to the distress of others and are more motivated to act on it because they have processed and personalized the experience of the person in distress [again, the mirror effect comes to play here] but it still doesn't fully address the issue. However, I am willing to take that 8 percent bigger amygdalae they discovered.

This final research took theory from the lab into what I can best describe as 'hooey' waters. But it does make sense. Especially since it is coming from a <u>professor of psychology</u>. The first research I discussed here focused on the mirror effect. This research focused on what they called the mirror-touch synesthesia. According to the article I read, this is a phenomenon where the line between what is actually experienced and what is witnessed is blurred. In other words, what you see and what you feel are almost the same thing. Now mirroring the pain of another person is a fairly common experience. As a guy, you see a guy getting punched in his nether region can inspire a knee jerk reaction from you. Even girls can have the same reaction. However, the lines begin to blur when you don't just physically react to the pain of this person but you experience a corresponding pain in your nether region as well. The guys who conducted this research say that it is so rare that only about 2 percent of the population experience this.

This got me really interested because I have had a personal experience that I would say fit into this phenomenon. This was this period that I went to visit one of my very close cousins. I spent a few days at their home and the wife was very pregnant at the time. It was not one of those celebrity type pregnancies with the glowing skin and all-round gorgeousness. She had morning sickness, back pain, and acne on her face and body. I felt so sorry for her that at the end of my first day, I was puking a lot. At first, we thought that I had come down with the flu or something. I was quarantined in my room but at the end of day two, it was clear that I was mirroring her symptoms as I suddenly had acne on my face and chest. This was an isolated incident and I never gave it much thought after that period. But reading up on this research brought that to mind. Anyway, back to the research.

The gist of it was that they handed out materials to random people to assess their empathy levels and then a short test was conducted on them. The test was pretty straight-forward. The subject was to sit down and then a finger would tap one side of their face while they watched another person being tapped on their face also except it is on the opposite side. Then they were asked where they felt the tap. The general theory is that people who have the mirror-touch synesthesia were hesitant in responding because they were unsure where they felt the tap. Now the results were not entirely conclusive in supporting the existence of empaths. However, they showed us an aspect of empathy that may explain why certain people are highly 'empathic' than others. The inability to distinguish between one's own personal experience from that of others is a disturbing concept and clearly needs to be studied further but it does highlight the traits. My major takeaway from the results of that research is that there is an element of choice in the process. There isn't a brain design flaw that makes you more or less prone to being empathetic. And I think that all three types of research in a way support this. A part of you will react to certain situations a little differently than other people would but at the end of the day, this is not something you are doing without the participation of your will. In other words, empaths are not born empaths. It is a process. A combination of your upbringing, personal values and sometimes, a touch of biology.

That said, I did promise to look at one of the not so conventional scientific explanation behind the existence of empaths. I read a lot of articles on the subject and this particular one stood out for me. According to them, [I am not even going to waste your time by sending you over there with a link to read it] empaths are people who suffer from sensory processing disorder. If you spilled your coffee as you read that, you would be forgiven. But brace yourself, there is more. You see, they believe that empaths are people who are unable to accurately sort through the experiences that they get from the world around them because they are so sensitive to everything from sights to sounds and even smells. To paraphrase, "when life gets too overstimulating...some people even report dizziness, as well as increased anxiety". I had a very hard time relating to this as I am sure you would too. But after reading their description of empathic behaviors, it made sense that this would make sense to them. According to them [paraphrasing again], "enhanced empathy is the emotional equivalent of feeling pain at the gentlest touch on your arm". I would file this under 7234 things that an empath is not.

In conclusion, according to science, being an empath does not make you an oddball. You may react to things differently but that is just a part of what makes you special.

The Difference Between Cognitive, Emotional and Compassionate Empathy

When I started this journey a few years back to try and get a clear definition of what being is and what it should mean to me, I was fortunate to meet some amazing people in the process. One of them was and remains to this day a very good friend of mine. I meant Austin back in my college years right after I had come to a conclusion about science being unable to dispute the existence of empaths, the next step was to figure out how to get a handle on the whole thing and by that, I mean understanding us better. This friend of mine said one of the most profound things about being an empath. He said being an empath is like having a neural link to everyone you meet, see, hear or know about. Of course, it was a very nerdy thing to say but it was profound nonetheless. Empaths are connected to people by their emotional experiences. If this is the case, are all empaths cut from the same cloth? I mean, what happens to the empath with all these connections? How do they react? Do they experience things the same way? These questions got us thinking, if there is nothing scientifically that can differentiate one empath from another, there has to be a way to get to understand what makes empaths in general tick. And we started exploring the behavior of empaths.

Empaths react to emotions but how they react is what makes them unique. In my research, there are several types of empathy but I am going to focus on three different types (we will look at a few others later). And from these differentiations, I believe we are able to find the answers to why we act the way that we do. I will explore and explain each type one after the other and then we would bring it back to how all of that correlates with what we know about empaths.

Cognitive Empaths

These are empaths whose empathic abilities are tied to perspective. For them, the empathic experience has more to do with the fact that they are able to see things from the view of the person that they are empathizing with. Of all the three types of empathy I have come across, I think that cognitive empathy is the most detached form of empathy (well as detached as an empath can be) and it is also the most passive form of empathy. Empaths who fall in this category would make excellent mediators or diplomats as they have a propensity to see the view from both sides of the fence.

People who don't understand cognitive empaths think that they are logical emotionless beings who stick to the facts and ignore everything else but the opposite is the case. When these guys tell you that they understand how you feel, you better believe them because they actually do. Beyond emotions, a cognitive empath makes genuine effort to really "get" where you are coming from by deliberately taking a mental work in your shoes. And when they are in those shoes, they immerse themselves in the situation so that they can feel everything that you are feeling. I think that their response to people's emotional distress is less reactive and more pragmatic. And not pragmatic in the general sense of the word. Their practical approach to a solution would stem from their clear vision of where you are coming from.

For example, when a cognitive empath is proffering a solution to say a homeless person, it is going to go beyond a can of soup. And this is because they see the problem as a whole and not just the momentary discomforts that the person is currently experience. A typical cognitive empath would put themselves in the entire journey of a homeless person. They would look at the migration pattern of the homeless person, look at the weather conditions of the areas they are most likely going to spend the night, the hassle of moving around from place to place but without the luxury of having assorted clothes to match the seasons. So, you would find them doing something like buying or even designing a flexible outfit that can adapt to different weather conditions without requiring much maintenance. Not many people would this decision but after reading up on them, it made sense that the solution would be so practical but born from a place of understanding.

Emotional Empathy

This type of empathy is pretty much self-explanatory but to ensure that we are all on the same page, I am going to get into it anyway. Emotional empathy is an instinctive form of empathy where the empath reacts to the emotions of other people. Psychological profilers refer to this type of empathy as the most primitive form of empathy. If you go over what we discussed in the section that focused on the scientific theories behind empathy, that mirror effect that was highlighted in one of the studies is very applicable here.

An emotional empath may mirror the emotion that they see or hear in other people. But their emotional reaction does not always come from a place of logical understanding. It is just a reflex. However, just because it does not appear to be a thought-out process does not mean that emotional empaths are clueless about their reactions. As a matter of, the emotional quotient of emotional empaths is unusually high. They would be having a conversation with you and based their interpretation of certain body languages and the vibes (for lack of a better word) that you give off, they can pick on what you are feeling and mirror either the same emotion or a corresponding emotion that would make you feel better. The general scope is that these guys are very emotionally intelligent.

One very common misconception people have about emotional empaths is that they are very emotional and would probably cry or lose control of their emotions at the drop of the hat. The reality is different. Their emotional intelligence affords them the ability to also sense their own emotions and then put a stopper on it before it gets out of hand. They can accurately detect emotions, reflect those emotions and sometimes even deflect those emotions before the person experiencing them even realizes what is going on. They have this innate gift of being able to make the people around feel better.

Compassionate Empathy

Now, this right here is the most active form of empathy. It combines aspects of both the cognitive empathy and the emotional empathy in that the compassionate empath is able to see things from the other person's point of view and then react based on the understanding that they now have. The emotional empath is the guy that we all know and have stereotyped as the typical empath while the compassionate empath is the one who we are all trying to become. The qualities of the compassionate empath almost put them on that celestial level because they sound almost too good to be true but that is who they are essentially.

An compassionate empath is the kind of person who would know that her best friend's heartbreak playlist is a sign that all in not well in the romance department and more than just acknowledging that this is what is going on, they would take it a step further by organizing just the right kind of event or activity that would get the said friend out of their funk and into a new groove. We all want a compassionate empath in our corner because they make life that much easier to navigate.

Now looking back on these three empaths, you would see that they each have their advantages and disadvantages (some more than the other) but they all serve a purpose. The end goal for empaths is to become the compassionate empath because they seem to have a healthy balance of action and reactions. One thing I observed across the board is that you can work towards improving aspects of yourself if you feel that you lean too much in one category. For instance, if you find that you are too pragmatic in your dealings with people, you may want to train yourself to be more emotionally intelligent. Don't get me wrong. I don't think that being practical is wrong. But sometimes, you can get a little too disconnected from the present reality because you are so focused on the bigger picture. A little emotional intelligence would go a long way in fixing this. As for the emotional empath, sometimes, the people around you are going to need more than a show of feelings to get them through situations. Getting to understand what they are really going through rather than relying on your instincts alone can help you be more 'useful' in times of crisis.

What makes an empath?

At the end of the first segment in this chapter, there was one big lesson we learned about what empaths are not… they are not created even though in some cases, they are born the way they are (very confusing, I know= but we will get to that in a bit). Granted, there are some biological markers that would play a role in how you process certain things, however, it does not ultimately define you. One of the biological factors attributed to certain empathic behaviors is the amygdalae. The science guys tell us that empaths have their amygdalae a little bit bigger than those of their average counterpart but there has also been some talk about people with larger amygdalae having deep seethed anxiety issues. According to that research, certain events (related to fear and anxiety) can trigger a growth of new cells in this area of the brain which in turn increases the size of this part of the brain leading to more anxiety. Seeing as empaths are not exactly riddled with anxiety, you can't blame biology for this one.

Some people try to trace their empathic abilities to a particular event, trauma or memory in their lives despite the fact that they are unable to remember a time when they were never the way they are now. Admitting to abilities being caused or triggered by some kind of tragedy would imply that the abilities were dormant and somehow, they were woken. Not only does this sound unrealistic, but it also sounds like something that was ripped off the plot of a low-budget sci-fi movie… cryptic, bizarre and false. If nothing else, the opposite happens. A tragic event can trigger a shut down of your empathic abilities. In subsequent chapters, we will discuss this in detail but take it from me, empathy is not born out of one's personal experience. I should point out here that there are certain experiences you would have that would cause you to empathize with anyone who goes through something similar. However, as I am sure we have learned so far, the display of empathy is not what automatically makes you an empath. There is more to it than that.

Until scientific research proves otherwise, rather than looking for one element as the spark that set off the who empathic nature in motion, think of your existence as the result of many factors coming together to create one awesome you. There is a biological component there to kick things off, a smidgen of experiences to open you up to more emotions, a little bit of social conditioning and a healthy dose of willpower.

5 other types of empaths you didn't know about

When we got into this segment about the different types of empaths, I did say we would look at other types of empaths. If you were unable to identify with the other forms of empathy, there is a great chance that you just might find your fit here. Mind you, these types of empaths are not very common but they have very unique identifiable traits and I will go over those traits briefly.

Geomantic Empath: The emotions of a geomantic empath is attuned to the environment that they are in. Their empathic abilities feed off the energies of whatever location they find themselves in. A typical geomantic empath would tell you that certain places make them feel a specific kind of emotion. They are usually drawn to places that either has a rich history or places that are considered sacred like temples, churches and so on.

Plant Empath: These guys have what we all call a green thumb and this is because plants always seem to thrive better under their care. But that has more to do with their natural intuition for the needs of the plants than their knowledge about planting itself. Plant empaths tend to thrive in jobs or businesses that revolve around the plant industry.

Animal Empath: Like the plant empaths, animal empaths are attuned to the needs of animals. They can somehow sense what animals need. The common term for them is animal whisperers. However, unlike plant empaths who connects with almost all kinds of plants, animal empaths are likely attuned to a specific animal. So, it is not out of the ordinary to find animal empaths whose empathy is towards cats, dogs or even birds.

Intuitive Empath: Also called claircognizant empaths, these guys can intuitively pick up on the emotions of other people without being told about them. They are the kind of empaths who are not easily swayed by the emotional expressions of people because they can sense the true nature of the person's emotions hidden underneath the façade that they present no matter how well constructed it is.

Physical/Medical Empath: A medical empath can almost immediately sense when a person's body is out of order for health reasons. They pick up on the energy coming off people that they meet and they can read that energy the same way a meteorologist would read the weather.

Chapter Three - The Empath Reality

After looking at empathy and the empath from both a mythical and scientific point, it is time to get real with what this is all about. And by real, I mean getting to the nitty-gritty details of the everyday life of an empath. Beyond the digital hype that has been amplified by the media's portrayal of empaths, there is the reality and it is not always pleasant. This reality is the reason you probably picked up this book in the first place. The 'gift' of seeing the world through the multi-colored lenses of emotions comes at a price. And the sooner you understand the price you are paying, the easier it would be to stop the spiral down the proverbial rabbit hole. As you read further, you may have to confront some startling truths. It may get a little uncomfortable but I promise you that it gets better in the end. Instead of looking at this as a forecast of doom, think of it as your private coming out party where you get to see yourself reflected in the pages of this book in all of your shining glory... flaws, strengths and all.

The Dark Side of Being an Empath

We know that empaths are generally emotionally intuitive on some level even if what they are attuned to might be different. However, this experience leaves them emotionally raw and sensitive most of the time. But emotional sensitivity is not the only thing that they have to deal with. Reflecting on my life as well as the information I was able to put together during my research, I made a list of a few of the things that almost all empaths would struggle with.

1. Empaths have a tendency to become depressed: For empaths, it is a constant battle to sort through the myriad of emotions that they feel. First, they have to work hard at keeping their emotions in check. As I have established, most empaths are emotionally intelligent and as a result, you won't find them losing control of their emotions but what most people do not realize is how difficult it is to do this. After putting a lid on their emotions, the next thing they have to do is determine if the emotions that they are struggling with is their own in the first place. Given their ability to absorb the emotions of other people, it is understandable that those feelings can eventually become mixed up with their own personal opinions and emotions. These frequent internal battles can lead to depression.

2. Empaths are typically emotionally exhausted: Dealing with emotions at the frequency and intensity that empaths do is very draining. This leads to an emotional fatigue

3. Empaths treat themselves as second class citizens: I am not sure if this is tied to the depression or the fact that they are always at the brink of exhaustion. But most empaths operate their personal lives on reserve because of all the other stuff that they have to deal with. Their impulsive need to help other people make it difficult for them to prioritize themselves.

4. Empaths struggle with guilt: Helping people is primal instinct for empaths. When they are confronted by any emotional puzzle, they have an almost compulsive need to put the pieces together and, in a situation where they fail to do so, they take this as a personal loss. They feel that they have failed the person or persons involved and this guilt could eat at them for a very long time. Sometimes, they task themselves with making up for this perceived failure by bending over backward to please and appease the "wronged" person.

5. Empaths are emotional sponges: Soaking up the energy of a room might sound cool until you find yourself soaking up more negative energy than a person should have to deal with. And while empaths have the ability to turn off the emotional faucet just as fast as they turn it on, their guilt-ridden nature makes them more inclined to deal with the negative stuff that people put out for longer than the average human. Coping with negative people is one thing but taking on some aspects of that negativity, that is a different ball game entirely and not a fun one at that. This brings us to the next big issue.

6. Empaths have a tendency to be in toxic relationships: Every one of the traits that we have looked at so far bring s us to this point. Because of the giving nature of the empath, they tend to attract the kind of people who would deliberately take advantage of that. And even when an empath is in a relationship where they are being taken advantage of, you would be hard-pressed to find them getting out of that situation willingly. Some of those who have successfully left those relationships end up guilt-tripping themselves back into those toxic situations.

These dark traits attributed to empaths does not essentially mean that all empaths have to be this way. In other words, you don't have to live with the darkness. However, there are certain behavioral patterns that have to be dealt with in order to deal with the darkness. Being an empath may make you prone to certain things like the depression we talked about but there are habits that you have that could drive your life to the point where everything that you do is characterized by depression. In this next segment, we are going to be looking at some of those habits.

5 Bad Habits that Empaths Must Let Go

1. Saying yes to everything: Empaths are natural people pleasers. This makes them more inclined to say yes even when that yes does not benefit them in any way. In the workplace, this can leave the empath stuck in a career rut as they find themselves spending more hours completing other people's project instead of focusing on growing their careers.

2. The need to fix everything: The phrase, "if it is not broke, don't fix it' tends to fly over the head of an empath. A bird with broken wings needs to be nursed back to health, a child with a sad history needs a little light to let go of that dark past but a grown person with deep anger

management issues need to make the choice to be better and no amount of loving or caring can get them to that place without their own consent. Empaths need to know when to leave things well alone.

3. Not speaking up for themselves: Empaths are no pushovers. At least not in the basic sense of it. However, they like to leave the floor open to other people to air their views and feelings while their own feelings are out in the back burner. This is born out of goodwill as they feel that the other person venting would help them release whatever they are feeling but it becomes a burden if you as an empath frequently have to hold back on saying how you really feel. This leads to a lot of repressed emotions which we know is a mental ticking time bomb.

4. Choosing to spend more time in their head: It is okay to step back every other day and take a few moments to be with yourself. But when it becomes a regular habit, it can be detrimental to you. It actually makes sense that you want to avoid dealing with all those emotions which come as part of the package when you have to deal with people. However, if you let go of most of the habits listed here, you would find it a lot easier to deal with people.

5. Taking things too personally: When you are sensitive and are an emotional sponge, everything that happens around you may begin to feel like it is all about you. Certain harmless comments or actions may be interpreted as a vendetta directed at you. I would say that has a lot to do with your need to piece together emotional puzzles, therefore, everything would seem connected to something which is then translated into personal meaning. But the truth is, things happen simply because they just happen.

The 5 Common Health Problems of Empaths

For the most part, due to the highly emotional nature of an empath, their health struggles are more psychological and mental than they are physical. So, a lot of things you would see in this segment have more to do with the mental illnesses than anything else. However, the lifestyle of the empath could influence the health issues they face more than their nature as empaths. Still, we cannot ignore the role that their nature plays in the process.

1. Anxiety: Most empaths battle with anxiety. The level of anxiety that they suffer varies from mild to severe and emotional empaths tend to have the most severe cases of anxiety when compared to others. Physical empaths are another group of empaths whose anxiety levels soar through the roof especially if they have to deal with crowds but it often veers into another mental health territory like panic disorders and we will get to that in a bit. Their ability to overcome or at least manage their anxiety is largely dependent on their self-awareness about who they are.

2. Depression: Given their propensity to juggle emotions at the same time, it is not surprising that they also have to deal with issues of depression from time to time. When they are not picking up on other people's emotions, they have to deal with guilt, isolation and their own personal drama. It is almost as if they can't catch a break. In addition to being self-aware, empaths need to talk with fellow empaths or therapist to help them sort through their emotions.

3. High Blood Pressure: High blood pressure is strongly linked to lifestyle and diet. However, stress and anxiety (which we know empaths are prone to) have been known to cause temporary spikes in blood pressure. The effect of anxiety on blood pressure does not last long but if it happens regularly, this blood pressure spikes can go ahead to cause damage to major organs in the body. Empaths should learn relaxation techniques that would help them bring their blood pressure down when they have an anxiety attack. Also, they need to watch out for the kind of habits they pick up to cope with anxiety. Habits like smoking can go on to complicate their health.

4. Panic Disorders: This usually happens when a person's stress and anxiety levels experienced are soaring really high. This is brought on by stressful situations and for empaths, this typically means when they

are surrounded by a lot of people with all of these emotions hitting them from different directions. Panic disorders are not necessarily life-threatening but the experience is horrible. Seeking the help of a medical professional goes a long way in the treatment and management of panic disorders.

5, Agoraphobia: Everyone has some form of phobia but there are phobias that are peculiar to people with certain traits. Agoraphobia is a form of anxiety that causes a person to be afraid of being in crowded spaces or places where they get a sense that they cannot escape. Agoraphobia is best treated in its early stages. The more it is left unattended, the more overpowering it comes. It is not life-threatening in the physical sense but it can rob you of living a fulfilled life. The experience is so much worse for an empath.

As you have read, the health issues of an empath are somewhat interrelated. Again, your lifestyle does play an important role in how healthy you are. But having a very good understanding of your personality as an empath and being very self-aware as to how things really work for you would go a long way to helping you establish a good foundation for a healthy life. As you have seen, prevention is way better than treatment for most of the ailments here. The general assumption is that it is specific situations that trigger these ailments and while that is true, that is not the only trigger out there. There are people who are classified as 'toxic' especially for an empath. These people are not necessarily evil but their behavior, mannerisms and personality traits make the life of an empath more complicated than it should be. So, in keeping with the theme of prevention, let us look at a few personalities you should definitely avoid as an empath.

The Personalities that Empaths Can't be Around

Narcissists:

These personality types are so into themselves that they would fail to see the harm their neglect and selfishness is causing the empath in their lives. Their actions may not be out of malice but the sensitive empath should not have to deal with this daily. It becomes even worse when the person is an abusive narcissist.

Manipulators:

This is another breed of selfish personalities who are willing to go the extra mile to make the people around them do the things that they want to do even if those things benefit no one else but themselves. Manipulators would play on the guilt that empaths feel to get them to do their bidding. This creates a very toxic cycle for the empath.

Abusers:

Nobody should be around abusers but this is especially true for empaths. Most abusers combine the traits of a narcissist and a manipulator in addition to their personal insecurities and constant need for control. An empath is actually the one person who can connect well enough with an abuser to even see things from their perspective and in a sad way, understand where they are coming from well enough to dare, I say it, justify the abuse that they are suffering. No one should have to go through that.

Chapter Four - The Injured Empath

In the first chapter, I shared some of the biggest misconceptions that people have about empaths. One of them was the idea that empaths are broken people; that for them to be able to connect to the feelings and experiences that a lot of people have, they must have walked the same path. By now, you know that this isn't the case. An empath does not need to have a first-hand experience to truly understand what you feel. However, through their abilities, they can get front row seats to your pain and know exactly how it feels. That said, it does not mean that there are no broken empaths. Being broken is part of the human experience and as long as you are human, you are bound to have a phase where you are broken. The loss of something of value whether an object, a person or even ideas that we have can cause a pain so intense that you feel crushed by the weight of it. This is the point where a person gets broken.

There is absolutely nothing wrong in being broken. The problem comes when you let that experience characterize everything that you do going forward. You have to understand that it is a human nature to fall, but it is also our nature to rise. Now rising does not necessarily mean that everything would right back to status quo. When you fall down and get injured, it hurts. Physiologically, a few cells die in the area where the injury occurred. But as the body begins the healing process, a few new cells are born. As the healing progresses, the pain begins to recede until all that is left to remind you of the injury is the scar. In the same manner, when life kicks us down, we get hurt and broken. But if you let it, the brokenness heals as begin to rise. However, we are left with the scars of those experiences. If the memories from those experiences are not brought into focus and the emotions that were stirred at that point in time not addressed, the emotional scars that will develop can affect the quality of life as well as the opportunities that you have later on.

An injured person is one carries the emotional scars from their past wherever they go. For an injured empath, the experience is even worse they are relieving these emotions at intensity levels that are so high that the past would seem like it only just happened yesterday. Each moment brings them a visit from the past and cages them in the present so that they are oblivious to the joys that are going on and unable to move forward to the future that they deserve. Injured empaths are curiously like the Mimosa Pudica also known as the touch me not plant. The second you touch them; their leaves close up. Incidentally, another nickname for the touch me not plant is 'the sensitive plant'. Their reaction to touch is the same way that an injured empath would react to life. Their emotional scars are so deep and the effect is so intense that every time life singles them out for a new experience whether good or bad, they quickly recoil to the 'safe' haven that they have created for themselves. The sad part is that this so-called safe haven is anything but safe. It is like a room with a living breathing nuclear reactor in it that draws its energy from the darkness surrounding it.

Another sad fact is that like the average person, most empaths won't even realize what is happening to themselves until either they are consumed by their past (an emotional nuclear explosion) or something disrupts the cycle of behavior that led down that destructive path, to begin with. It doesn't help that the coping mechanisms for most empaths are self-destructive behaviors, to begin with. For starters, there is that reclusive behavior. There is nothing wrong in being a recluse, but you take things to the extreme when paranoia sets in and you begin to hide even from your own shadow. The only way forward is to allow our minds to heal and recover from the emotional injuries sustained. When a physical wound is being treated, the very first thing any doctor would do is to make an attempt to treat the life-threatening symptoms of the wound. For emotional injuries, I would say the equivalent of that is coming out of your shell. Even if you are going to stay inside of your house cooped up, the least you can do is to pick up the phone and call somebody and then just talk. It does not have to be about what you are going through. The fact that you are having a conversation alone is going to be like coming up for a breath of fresh air after in an oxygen-deprived space.

The next step is to go the source of the wound which in the case of an empath is not always the incident that you think triggered the pain in the first place. It is usually something called compassion fatigue. And that is what the rest of this chapter is going to be about.

What is Compassion Fatigue?

In very lay terms, compassion fatigue happens when a person becomes emotionally desensitized to the needs, pains and sufferings of other people. Compassion fatigue is also known as secondary traumatic stress and has been associated with people who have been constantly exposed stories and experiences of tragedies for so long that it would appear as though their nerve endings just snapped and stopped functioning. Now, you may be inclined to think that this means the person experiencing the compassion fatigue (in this case an empath) would move from their end of the scale and tip towards the section where you have the psychopaths. This is not so. People who suffer from compassion fatigue don't suddenly become dead to their emotions. In fact, they become even more acutely aware of it. what happens is that they internalize these emotions that they feel and are unable or unmotivated to act on it.

Let me give you a brief rundown of my theory on the subject. When you are confronted with a situation where a person that you know on some level is going through a very tragic experience, you are instinctively inclined to want to help. You find a way to provide a solution for that person. Even if you cannot completely avert the tragedy, you want to do all that you can to improve the situation. When you achieve this, there is a reward section of your brain that is triggered. You feel very good about this good deed that you are done. In that moment, the sun shines a little brighter, the world appears to have a little more color and life, in general, is very fantastic. This perhaps explains people have been trying to convince us that doing good does some with its own special kind of reward. This is all good and well. After living through this wonderful experience which essentially is a psychological feedback from your good deed, you are inclined to repeat this process again. It doesn't matter if the circumstances are the same or different, you want to help this new person. For empaths, this experience can be very addictive. They want to keep doing these good deeds and continue reliving the psychological aftermath. It is like a high except that there is no drug that can quite match the effect. But when happens when the good deed that you carried out is unable to make a difference?

This is where the story takes a slightly darker turn. Let us take this same scenario we mentioned earlier but with a not so positive outcome. You are confronted with a situation where someone you know on some level is going through some kind of tragic experience. As a good friend, colleague or whatever your relationship is with that person, you step in to help because that is just what you do. Now you offer this help in the hope that the tragedy can be averted or in the very least, the circumstance can be improved but instead, nothing happens. Or even worse, things become even more tragic than you met them. You are now forced to watch this person live through the pain and trauma from their experience until it either ends their life or ends your relationship with them. As an empath, you would get some feedback from their pain and this registers on your psyche. It doesn't stop you from trying to help people but there is a part of you that struggles with the following;

1. Your failure to help this person
2. Your second-hand experience of their pain

3. Your anxiety losing another friend or relationship in the same way

Things get a little more complicated for empaths who work in specific professions where they are constantly faced with tragedy. For empaths who have to deal with this occasionally with their circle of friends, the progression of compassion fatigue is slower. But for people whose occupations are in the health sector like nurses, care-givers, psychology and so on, there is a high risk of developing compassion fatigue within a shorter timeframe. People who work as lawyers as also susceptible to it. Empaths in these fields sometimes end up being unable to differentiate their work life from their personal lives to you would find the emotional burn out affection their ability to connect emotionally with other people too.

Having all of this in mind, you cautiously approach other relationships. Now, we all know that at some point, life happens. This other relationship may not have the same tragic elements as the previous but even the slightest hint at tragedy might get your instincts kicking in on overdrive. Obviously, you rush in to help. This time around, you are just as anxious about the results of your efforts as you are about the person's wellbeing that even if your effort is rewarded by an aversion of tragedy, your only psychological reward would be relief that all works out. The rush is not the same this success would seem to highlight your failure. And this drives you into a cycle where you keep trying to make up for the proverbial one that got away. If your effort to help fails like the first time around, you are flung deeper into that cycle and anxiety takes deeper roots in your psyche. The more fixes and saves you do, the more you want to do, but this is no longer inspired by the high which we talked about initially. It is now about balancing the scales. The stress and anxiety that comes with each case that you face pushes you closer to the line where it is no longer about helping people but simply getting through the day. At this point, you are having secondary traumatic stress.

Signs of an Injured Empath

The point where an empath experiences compassion fatigue is where the emotional injury we discussed earlier is rooted. As I said, it is not isolated to an event or a singular experience so you cannot take a mental trip to this specific spot, snap your fingers and find closure. It is a little more complicated than that. Thankfully, you can determine if you have arrived at this point even though you don't know what led you here. If you recall, I painted a picture of a safe haven likened to a room housing an active nuclear reactor and how toxic that environment can be for you. In this section, we are going to highlight all these factors that make being in the state where you are dangerous and then we will talk about how to cross those hurdles.

1. A Keen Sense of Hopelessness that Results in Detachment

If you find yourself unable to summon a genuine feeling of optimism for the things that you do, you may have subscribed to that feeling of hopelessness. When you have a situation that requires your help and you do it not because you are certain or in the very least hoping that it would make a difference, but because you are obligated to, you might be having compassion fatigue. In this case, the need to play out your role takes priority over the needs of the person. Everything about caring for this person becomes a routine activity for you. The biggest clue in this regard would be the fact that you are unable to look past today because you feel that there is a very strong possibility that there won't be a tomorrow.

2. Apathy Toward the People You Care for

This is a form of detachment but not necessarily an absence of care because as an empath on some level, you always care. But the experiences you have had has groomed you to the point that you have become indifferent to the entire experience. You are more matter-of-factly in the way you care and help. Since your indifference does not come from a place of malice or ill will, you will always show up.

However, your indifference has been constructed as a wall to protect you from the tragedy you are already expecting so that 'when' it happens, you are not so visibly affected by it. If you find yourself thinking this way, know that you are probably experiencing compassion fatigue

3. Elevated Stress Levels

In the face of tragedy, we experience a lot of things emotionally. These emotions cause stress. Now there is the normal stress level of the average person and then you have abnormal stress levels. Compassion fatigue triggers a high level of stress even in situations that have very little similarities to the events that you can call the ground zero of your emotional trauma. In addition to all the other symptoms mentioned here, if you discover that you are reacting adversely to stress such as breathlessness, inability to focus, severe anxiety and panic attacks, you are having compassion fatigue

4. Nightmares and disruption in sleep routines

Nightmares and a change in sleep routine is typically a sign of an internal struggle with some kind of unresolved emotional trauma. When dealing with the pain of other people trigger nightmares and sleeplessness, it is possible that you are having an emotional burnout. Your mind is unable to cope with the situation and even worse, it is unable to cope with the fact that you cannot cope with the situation... a classic nightmare for empaths.

5. Struggling with feelings of Self-Contempt

Empaths already have a thing for guilt-tripping themselves. When they hit the compassion fatigue point, this guilt grows into self-contempt as they feel a sense of disappointment in their inadequacies. This is because empaths measure their sense of self-worth with their ability to provide help and 'fix' things. Failure to do this causes self-doubt which evolves into guilt and grows into contempt.

If you look at all of the symptoms listed, you would see the progression of the internal struggle brought on by compassion fatigue. An outward experience becomes an inward struggle that becomes all about them which can be pretty selfish and a strong contradiction to their normally selfless nature. The inward struggle is what keeps them in that 'room' we talked about earlier. They find it difficult to come of this mental space that they have created because they have adorned themselves with the persona of a victim. Somehow, this thing that totally was about them has now made them the victim. In the next chapter, we discuss this in detail.

Beware: The Victim Complex

Self-pity is a normal experience for everyone. We have moments when we fall into that woe-is-me hole but as long as you don't hold on to that hat for longer than necessary, you are going to be fine. Victim complex, on the other hand, is choosing to lay on a bed of misery, covering up yourself with your failures or the list of everything that has gone wrong and just lying there in it. For an empath, having a case of compassion fatigue can create a segue into a full-blown victim complex experience. The general experience of the victim complex would see the person experiencing it deferring all responsibility to everyone and everything but themselves. But in the case of the empath, they take the whole blame for everything and then somehow make the entire experience about them. I know that this seems a little confusing but let me explain it anyway.

An empaths victim complex is not about making themselves the star of the show by abdicating any blame or responsibility that was assigned to them. They don't wear the sad-is-me crown to make other people feel sorry for them. If anything, they would hate to be that person because there is a very strong possibility that they deal with such people on a regular basis. The victim complex for empaths come in when they internalize their failures, store up the pain that they have absorbed on the outside and then sort of idolize it on the inside. Most injured empaths have a victim complex. They do not have the resilience needed to cope with their personal failures. Now let me digress a little bit here. A personal failure for an empath goes beyond their inability to successfully complete a project. That kind of failure is one that they can deal with. But when they are unable to fix their people projects, that kind of failure seeps deep into their minds and they take it personally. They can get so fixated on it that they work twice as hard to 'redeem' themselves with other people projects.

Besides the increased risk of failure associated with taking on more people project, there is the problem of not dealing with the initial failure. As a result, any people project that is taken on would only echo the failure and the longer they deal with this, the more intense the situation would get. The intensity of the emotions experienced would lead to an emotional burn out that we have now identified as compassion fatigue which leads us to where we are now. A victim complex sounds like something harmless but here is the part I am pretty sure that you did not know. The victim complex is the element that keeps the wheels spinning in this self-destructive cycle. It is the bars that would keep you locked in that 'safe' room that stops you from living your life. I read of an ancient religious group where believers or practitioners were physically chastised whenever they err. These chastisements were so terrible that they would be in physical pain for months on end. The scars that they bore on their bodies told tales of horror and trauma so horrendous that you would think that they served in slaves camps or some kind of torture chamber. The reality was that all of these injuries were self-inflicted.

The need to make yourself pay for perceived failures by locking up yourself in this 'safe' haven is the emotional equivalent of the self-inflicted injuries on those believers. Take your freedom today by learning to prioritize your self-care just as much as you value the care of other people. Most importantly, you need to stop looking at people as projects that you need to fix. I have mentioned this before and later in the book, we would discuss this in-depth. But if you do anything today, let it be that you acknowledge your importance and treat yourself accordingly. That said, I would like us to look at another self-destructive behavior that could ruin the life of an empath

The Truth About Empaths and Addiction

The emotional turmoil, as well as the intrinsic nature of the empath, make them a perfect candidate for addiction. Their need to get out of their own heads every other day means they are open to trying out coping mechanisms that would offer them this. The fact that this emotional turmoil is an ongoing struggle means that they are more likely to keep going back to continue using this coping mechanism especially if it successfully provides the temporary fix that they need. When you try something for so long, it becomes a routine. Over time, a routine becomes a habit and with habits, especially bad habits, you get addicted. A coping mechanism could be anything from drug use to comfort eating to watching porn. And the thing with these things I have mentioned is that you never really see it as a problem until it is too late.

In my experience, food was my vice. It started out innocently enough. I would come back home from work, tired and exhausted. However, no matter how exhausted I was, sleep was something that eluded me. So, I would get out of bed, fix myself something sweet in the kitchen and then plop myself down on the couch and binge-watch those terrible television shows. In those moments, I was completely calm, very relaxed and certainly not thinking about the horrible day I had at work. After some time, I decided to upgrade my couch meal to something with a more 'luxurious' feel. I would stop by at the pastry shop on my way home and pick up an array of sweet treats and then repeat my routine in front of the TV. A few months later, the couch didn't feel comfortable enough so I got a larger screen and then took the show into my bedroom. For the better part of a year, I spent my nights eating junk food in bed while watching junk TV. As you can imagine, it started showing on my waistline. My old clothes stopped fitting me and then I started feeling more self-conscious about how I looked.

I had friends who were too polite to point out the physical changes but I could see the way they looked at me. Then I had 'friends' who had no problems telling me exactly how they felt. Their words made me feel even more horrible about myself and when I felt really bad, it meant I spent a lot more at the pastry shop. My lowest point which also turned out to be my turning point was this particular day when I was eating this really delicious donut on my way home (it had gotten to the point that I couldn't wait to get home anymore). The donut slipped from my hand and fell on the floor. It was probably around 7 pm and there weren't that many people on the street. I know because I glanced around and then I did the unthinkable. I bent down and pick my fallen donut off the sidewalk. I blew on it and ate it with I was still bent there with one knee on the floor. Just then, I caught my reflection in one of the storefronts and I did not like the person who was starring back at me. To make a long story short, I had a good cry when I got home and that was the beginning of my journey to this point where I am writing my story in a book. Today, I still have an addiction but I have made a conscious effort to ensure that my addiction is healthy. I have a habit for different moods. When I am angry, I paint. When I feel a little blue, I get on the treadmill or put on my boxing gloves and work up a good sweat. When I am anxious, I write.

You are going to have to find out what works for you but it starts with you admitting to yourself that this seemingly harmless habit you have engaged may not be entirely healthy for you. People think that drug is the only harmful addiction, I have read about empaths who are addicted to the misery they are facing that they would willingly self-sabotage any shot that they have at happiness. It is sad to witness but this is the reality. When you are experiencing those floods of emotions, what are the things that you do to cope? Do those things add value to you as they make you feel better or do they take away something valuable from you in exchange for making you feel better? Addiction for empaths is a serious problem and it needs to be taken seriously or else you would end up complicating things for yourself. Today, the goal is to get you out of that sense of false security that you have created for yourself. This book is a guide on how you can survive in the world as an empath. For that to happen, you need to step out of your enclave and into the real world because not only will you survive it, you will thrive in it.

Chapter Five - The Dangers of Being an Empath

In the previous chapter, we explored some of the dangers of being an empath. In this chapter we are going to delve into the dark side of things. Leading up to this point, empaths have been regarded as beings in possession of supernatural power. That is cool and I honestly wished it was that way 100% of the time but there's a price that empaths and it goes beyond the emotional struggles that we have. Because of the intricate nature of the empath, they tend to attract a certain kind of people to themselves. We have talked about the need for the empath to fix people. Whenever they encounter people with emotional struggles and some psychological pain, the first instinct is to want to help but we forget that not all the people that come to us want to be helped. Some people are programmed or to be more specific, they are emotionally programmed to take advantage of the help that we wish to offer and this is where the problem begins.

The empire's desire to help attract a specific kind of people and more often than not, these people fall into the category of those with a psychological need to take advantage of others. Sometimes these relationships start out with good intentions. But in time, their predatory nature quickly takes over and they end up destroying the empath from within. This is the danger that all empaths face. In the previous chapter, I talked about certain kinds of people that empaths should avoid and one of those people is the narcissist. The narcissist is a special breed of individuals and their qualities go beyond their love for themselves. They are recognized for their skills at masterfully manipulating people to do their bidding and the nature of the empath make them more prone to the manipulations of a narcissist.

Identifying a narcissist

Empath Survival Guide

From old literature, we are led to believe that a narcissist is someone who is vain; a person who is obsessed with their physical looks and how they present themselves to the world. In psychology, it's a lot deeper than that as narcissist take on a different form. One of their unappealing qualities is the fact that they have a great sense of self-importance but for someone who is not very observant, this attribute is not something that you would pick on right away. Their victim mentality provides a great mask for their true personality but more importantly, they have a way of blending in perfectly with the rest of the society which makes it somewhat difficult to identify them. Some narcissists are simply harmless in their relationships. Narcissists who fall in this category are people who are self-aware and have worked on the negative side of themselves. But then you have the narcissists on the other spectrum who are terrible as companions because their sense of self-importance is so grand that they are willing to compromise the feelings and emotions of other people just to satisfy their own needs. Narcissists are selfish, self-important and self-righteous but ironically, they are the list self-aware people.

Based on the description I have given, I am sure you can understand why narcissists are people that can be very difficult to deal with even for anyone who is not an empath. However, if you're able to understand them, you get a better sense of how to relate with them especially if you are an empath. According to psychology, there are different types of narcissists. You have the grandiose narcissist. These guys are basically people who have a huge ego. To deal with them, you need to offer up a lot of attention in the form of praise. This feeds their ego and makes them much more manageable in relationships. Then you have the vulnerable narcissists. You can identify them by the victim mentality that they seem to wear like a badge. Everything that happens in life seems to revolve around them. It could be raining somewhere in China and causing floods in certain villages but the vulnerable narcissist living a few continents away would find a way to make it about them. They have a very high tendency to complain about anything and everything. To manage a relationship with them, they need to be given attention in the form of emotional support. And then finally, you have the malignant narcissists. These guys are the ones you need to watch out for. The other two types of narcissist mentioned earlier can be emotionally exhausting to deal with but as far as damages go, as long as you can give them what they want in terms of their emotional needs, they are fine. Malignant narcissists, on the other hand, display a lack of empathy on the level that is so high that psychologists compare them with psychopaths.

To identify the malignant narcissist in your life you would need to be very attentive. As I said earlier, a narcissist has a way of blending in with everyone. So, there aren't really factors that make them stand out from the crowd. In fact, psychologists believe that narcissist are usually happier than most people who have been diagnosed with some form of psychological disorder. To keep things in perspective, I compiled a list that will help you identify a narcissist specifically, the malignant narcissist. This list is based on certain traits. Be guided though, you need a clinical psychologist to accurately diagnose a malignant narcissist but until that happens, here are few red flags that should make you wary of any person who displays more than one of these traits.

1. They have a strong sense of self-importance
2. They are very obsessed with their idea of what they consider as ideal (the ideal wife, the ideal friend, the ideal love, the ideal relationship)
3. They have a very strong sense of entitlement
4. They have an unrealistic expectation about things in general
5. They have a tendency to use other people to get what they want
6. They are very manipulative
7. They lack empathy and display an unwillingness to recognize the needs and emotions of other people

There is a general saying that opposites attract. Perhaps this is the foundation of the relationship between the narcissists and an empath, because, on a surface level, it is hard to determine why someone as sensitive and generous as an empath will fall for someone as cold and calculating as a narcissist but when you explore the dynamics of the relationship it does make sense why these 2 opposites would be attracted to each other. However, this relationship can only be described as a recipe for disaster. To better understand why this continues to happen, I felt it will be important to look at why these 2 people would choose each other and to determine that, we need to look at what each personality would stand to gain from this relationship.

Why Narcissists Are Drawn to Empaths

If you look at the traits of a narcissist, you would see that for them every relationship that they get into is a one-sided business transaction designed to favor just one party. I leave you with just one guess as to who that party is. A typical malignant narcissist is very calculating and they never enter into anything without a plan on how they can take. From the onset, they can instinctively recognize people who would give them a hard time achieving their goals. They hate people that they cannot manipulate and in the workplace, or environments where they are required to team up with other people, you would find the narcissist at loggerheads with these types of people. To look at what a narcissist would be drawn to, let us take a look at how relationships work with a narcissist.

When a narcissist likes someone, they would turn on their charm on them and for a brief moment, that person would feel like they are the most special people in the world. In this timeframe, the narcissist would push back gently to get a feel of their resistance level. The weaker it is, the more they push. In this stage, they would continue to maintain their charming façade. And then when they get to a point where they are absolutely certain that this person is enthralled with them, their sadistic nature and their real intentions would start to manifest. The charming exterior that they presented would either disappear completely or be used as a form of sick reward for behavior that they consider good. This relationship pattern would play out until either the narcissist gets tired or the empaths wake up from the spell that was cast over them. In some cases, it usually ends in tragedy. That said, let us look at those characteristics that act as a magnet for narcissists.

A narcissist is drawn to someone who;

- Is very giving emotionally and physically
- Has a tendency to put the needs of other people before their own
- Doesn't stand up to people they care about
- Is not anti-social but not very social either because of their shyness
- Has a very strong sense of loyalty
- Is emotionally sensitive and somewhat fragile
- Is easily moved to act on the emotional needs of others

If you noticed, these are all common traits of empaths.

Why Empaths are Drawn to Narcissists

Why do good girls like bad boys and why do the good guys fall for really bad girls? This is the question that comes to mind when I think of empaths going out with narcissists. But after being in a relationship like this, I understand why I went out with this person. Empaths are people fixers and we are naturally drawn to people that we think new can fix. The narcissist may turn on their charm to the max but on some level, I believe that an empath can always sense the damage underneath. And it is this damage that reels us in. We feed ourselves that we are going to be that special person who fixes them and makes them as right as rain. Every single gesture that is good and right towards us goes on to cement or affirm this illusion we have created and every struggle is interpreted one of the things that we have to tolerate until we hit our goals. If we dwell on this illusion long enough, the lines between reality and fiction become blurred and that illusion becomes a living breathing reality.

The primary attraction in all this for an empath has got to be the damage persona that we sense. And then the next thing would be our need to punish ourselves when we fail at our people projects. Except in this situation, the person meting out the punishment is the narcissistic figure in our lives. I think the last piece in this puzzle would be the fact that empaths feed off emotions and the ego of a narcissist feeds off people who feed off their emotion. This appears to be a symbiotic relationship in the most unhealthy way as one party is being fed with nourishments while the other party is getting toxins.

As an empath reading this, I am sure that you would have recognized a similar pattern of behavior that was exhibited in your previous or current relationship. For those whose previous relationship showed this pattern, be thankful that you dodged a bullet. If you need to talk to a psychologist to help you heal from the damage of that relationship (there will be damages) don't hesitate to speak to someone. Get closure, find yourself again and let it go. If this is your current relationship, it might be time for you to call it quits. This is not a healthy situation for you. If you have not yet been cut off from your friends and family that you trust (this is a classic narcissist move), you need to reach out to someone and ask for an intervention. In the very least, take a temporary break from this person. Don't expect this to happen without some negative reaction from the narcissist because his or her ego would be bruised and they would want to redeem it.

Signs an Empath is with an Emotional Vampire

If you're an outside the observing the relationship dynamics between an empath and a narcissist, it is not difficult to see where the hurt is coming from and where it is going. Narcissist are emotionally draining and yet the empath remains in that relationship anyway. Being an observer of my own past relationships, I can pinpoint the exact moment where I figured things were going terribly wrong. No matter how well a narcissist presents themselves, there are signs even from the beginning. You just have to be open-minded and let go of any illusions you may have. This is the hardest part but we will talk about this in the next segment. For now, let us look at those signs that can tell you immediately that the relationship you are in is destroying you from the inside.

1. You are fighting a solo battle

For starters, you want the growth of the person more than they do. There is a general saying there you can take the horse to the water but you cannot force it to drink. Individual growth is something that we have to desire for ourselves. Now, I get that as an empath, we get to see sides of a person that not many people see because we look inwards as opposed outwards. The problem is that the person we see on the inside is the person who they have a potential to become however we look at that as a reality and we commit ourselves to that illusion. If they can't see what you see, there is nothing that can be done to change things. Recognize this.

2. Everything in your relationship seems to be about them

A relationship is a two-way street. As long as they are 2 people involved, it is important that the needs, opinions, and feelings of the parties involved are recognized an attended too equally. Anything less would mean that one party is benefiting and the other party is suffering. Empaths have a tendency to be addicted to the suffering that is usually self-inflicted. This is difficult enough not to mention unhealthy to deal with on your own but if you are in a relationship and this is what you're going through, chances are you have an emotional vampire in your life who is leeching you for everything that you have. It may be time to check out of that relationship.

3. They have a general sense of entitlement

Just because you are in a relationship with someone doesn't mean that you owe them anything. People get together for mutually beneficial reasons however, there shouldn't be any sense of entitlement as to the fulfillment of those reasons. You are your own person. What you do with your time and how you do it is exactly your business. If anyone tries to force their needs on you, that is a red flag.

4. The arrogance of the person you are dealing with borders on a power play

Some people are generally arrogant we all have our pride and egos. But when a person becomes condescending in their behavior toward you, it becomes unhealthy. You deserve to be respected as a person and a relationship where there is no respect except when you are dealing with the opinions and thoughts of the other person changes from a loving union to a slave and master type situation.

5. Your social life is being controlled by the other person

As empaths, we have our periods of isolation. However, we are not introverts by choice. We always have that circle of friends or family or people that we connect with in general. The narcissist in our lives would work hard in ensuring that we are disconnected from those people that matter to us. For them, having an empath isolated from their social network would make them more malleable to their manipulations. They also feel like there are going to be fewer interruptions this way.

How to Stop Being a Target for Emotional and Energy Vampires

From my experience, the hardest word for an empath to say which coincidentally also happens to be the magic word that can go a long way to making life significantly better for them is the word, no. Apart from the ability to say no to people. I believe that by recognizing these signs which I listed above you are putting yourself on the right track to preventing yourself from getting into toxic relationships. Now that you can spot an abusive relationship, here are a few more things you can do to protect yourself;

1. Educate yourself on the concepts of an ideal relationship

Empires tend to get into their head when it comes to relationship. Like the narcissist, they project their own perception of a relationship. Unfortunately, it is often based on their personal experiences with people. This can be wrong because most times, their relationship with people tend to have this parasitic component where one person feeds off the other person. Healthy relationships don't work that way. Today, I urge you to read up on relationship materials; go on the Internet, read books and pay attention to the healthy couples in your life. Let the things that you discover help guide you to what a healthy and normal relationship is meant to look like.

2. Don't ignore your instincts

One of the wonderful gifts that we have as empaths is the ability to accurately read people, however, when our emotions are involved, we overlook the information our instincts are trying to pass them across to us. We ignore our guts and focus instead on the illusions we have built around the relationship and when this happens, even when we see physical red flags pointing us towards the toxicity of the relationship we still choose to remain. One of the many important things you are going to learn by the time you are done reading this book is that your instinct as an empath is powerful and it is also one of the guiding forces in your life. From this point on, you have to learn to pay attention to what the inner voice is saying.

3. Stop treating people as projects that need to be fixed

When we go into a relationship, we look at a person as a task to score us some mental points if we succeed in fixing them. When a person becomes a project, we fail to see the human element and oftentimes, that human element is the ability to go dark emotionally. Having that kind of mentality often gets us in trouble because when you cease to see a person as an actual person, you would be blinded to their potential to hurt you. You get caught up in the image you have created in your head. Your weakness is your deadly attraction to people who are damaged and emotionally unstable. Recognize this and make efforts to correct it as soon as possible.

4. Get to know a person before you decide to date them

A lot of mistakes can be avoided if you take the time to know the person that you are committing yourself to. They may present a false exterior initially, but with the time you have deliberately created to get to know each other, you can successfully peel off those layers and get to see them for who they really are. This is a Golden rule for every kind of relationship but it is especially important for empaths.

5. Teach yourself to desire the best

Most empaths feel that it is conceited to want or desire good things and this is understandable as it goes against their nature which puts everyone before themselves. But if you want to avoid toxic relationships it is important that not only are you able to recognize good things and good people, you should also capable of wanting those good things for yourself. You deserve happiness. Always remind yourself that no matter how much you give of yourself, you cannot make someone that is by nature bad become good. It is like drinking poison in the hope that by the time the poison gets to your stomach, it will turn into a refreshing drink. It does not make sense.

Chapter Six - Healing the Empath Heart

I am not the kind of person who likes to indulge in self-pity but I think in this place where we are right now, it would only be fair to recognize the emotional struggle that we all go through as empaths. After decompressing everything I did in the last chapter, it just feels like this is the right time to simply put a pause on everything and inhale... breath in the moment. Life really is beautiful. And we can only enjoy it if we can get out of our heads for a moment. Because I am an empath, I understand living outside our heads is not really a luxury we can afford especially since we have to deal with people and their emotions every other day. But that is fine. We need these emotions in other to feed the gift that we have on the inside, however, as we go through these emotions it is important to have a balance where we not only let go of the painful and hurtful things that we feel, we find a way to heal our hearts.

In the first chapter of this book, I talked about some of the misconceptions that people have about empaths. One of those misconceptions is the idea that empaths are broken people. Sometimes the pain that we carry is not our pain. Remember the mirror effect? These are feelings that we absorb from other people and if we don't deal with those feelings, we could end up with a crisis on our hands. What is the point of all of this? Healing in this sense does not necessarily mean that we are broken. Healing for us is a way to sort through the emotions; a way to relax and calm are in ourselves. Healing for an empath is more than just a biological activity brought on by pain. It is a pathway to our balanced emotional well-being.

5 Healing Activities for Empaths to Relax

There are different kinds of empaths (we have looked at more than a handful of them already) and the key to their healing usually lies in their intrinsic nature. For the compassionate empath, their road to healing could probably be found in activities that reward their need to help people. So, something as simple as serving soup in a homeless shelter would be relaxing. For physical empaths, activities that involve connecting with people especially when the focus of the connection is healing would be helpful. Such activities could be either a nice body massage or a Reiki healing session. For animal empaths, just spending a day indulging in a fun activity with their favorite pets can do a lot of wonders for their mental health. These things I have mentioned are unique to the nature of the empath

However, there are simple general activities that empaths can carry out that will bring them to that place where they can start to experience healing internally. If you take anything away from this chapter, let it be the fact that the healing of an empath is not initiated by a drug or the use of a substance no matter how mild. You don't need to start doing something that could become addictive. However, I created a list of 5 general activities that can help you get to a place of calm. Use this as a guide. The goal is that at the end of the segment, you would be able to relate with more than one or two activities on that list. Remember your emotional well-being is very important. If you are going to ever enjoy your gifts as an empath, you need to learn to relax.

1. Start journaling

Journaling is a therapeutic activity that you may not realize you need. It is an excellent way to get you out of your head. If you are observant, you may have noticed that I have used this phrase "get out of your head", a lot. What I mean is getting out of that mental space where you are constantly processing emotions. I know that as an empath you need to deal with different kinds of emotions at the same time. If you keep that process inside your head especially over a long period of time, chances are you're going to end up stressed out. Not many empaths have friends that they can talk to or people who will even understand what they're going through. A Journal enables you to write out your thoughts and sort through your feelings without having to deal with the backlash of processing those various emotions. it is a relaxing experience as it gives you focus and when you have focus, you are more in control of what you feel and how it affects you.

2. Release your inner artist

This part can be a little bit difficult to understand. But this is what I mean. When you are going through one of those emotional experiences, you can take that pain and turn it into art by engaging in activities that require you to be creative. This could be an activity like writing a poem, painting or something like woodwork. Now realize this, it is not about what you create. It is about the process. From experience, this process creates what I call transference of energy. That negative emotion you are feeling is converted into a creative process that has the potential to become an art. You don't have to aspire to do something grand (that would only aggravate the stress), it could be something as simple as splashing colors on a board or playing around with words. These are very cool ways to help you again, get out of your head

3. Champion a cause you care about

You know you want to make a difference and alleviate the sufferings of people. Taking a moment to give towards a cause that is important to you can have a relaxing effect on you. If you prefer to be hands-on, you can volunteer for a few minutes or hours (depending on your schedule). The helps you take care of your "people project" instinct while giving you some appropriate distance.

4. Change your routine

Empaths are creatures of habits. They feel safe in those routines even though those routines may not be good for their mental and physical health in the long run (remember my couch and pastry experience?). Breaking from routine might sound scary but when you take the step, the result can be elating. A word of caution though. Ensure that the new routine you are signing up for is beneficial to your mental health.

5. Meditation

This list would not be complete if there wasn't a mention of meditation. If you learn how to do it right, you can induce a state of complete calm no matter how stressed out you feel. Include words of affirmation as part of your meditation routine to make the meditation experience even more relaxing. I found my peace in Reiki, an energy healing journey that I take daily.

Steps to Heal Your Emotional Triggers

Emotional triggers are events, memories, places or even words that the second you see them, it invokes a specific kind of emotional reaction. When something happens to you, our brains create neural pathways (this is why having new experiences on a regular are good for you) and when those experiences are negative, the emotion that you experienced in that moment is registered and every time something similar happens, you are immediately transported to that moment. This is why you could perceive something like say a fragrance and you are transported to a time in your childhood when someone significant in your life did something while wearing that fragrance. The emotions triggered could be good or bad, this is determined by the experience that you had.

Obviously, you would be comfortable reliving good emotions unless it gets to a point where those memories are stopping you from moving forward with your life. Negative emotions affect us in many ways and those are almost never good. Personally, I think the only good thing that comes from negative experiences are the lessons that they provide. Whatever emotions are being triggered, the fact is that you are being held back from moving on and living your best life now. The best way forward is to do the following;

1. Stay in the moment

Stop taking a trip down memory lane. If an event occurs that makes you think of the past, don't hold on to it. Focus on what is happening. Don't let the emotions that they bring on hold you down and more importantly, don't look at your present as your opportunity to take revenge on your past. Address the situation as it happens.

2. Don't try to control the situation

Control is an illusion and if you buy into this illusion, you increase the stress and anxiety that comes with reliving emotional triggers. Accept that you cannot control what is happening to you, you cannot control anyone involved in the situation that is messing you up, however, your experience does not have to be determined by this thing that you are going through. It sounds like a contraction but here is what I mean. You have a choice in how you feel because that is what you have control over. The happiness or sadness you feel and how long you feel those things is determined by you. So, leave the situation but control your emotion.

3. Don't run from it

There is a saying that the splash of water you run away from today could become the pool that drowns you tomorrow. It might be painful to confront our feelings. But it is in that confrontation that you will encounter the truth and you already know what they say about the truth and freedom. And this brings us to the next point.

4. Know your truth

Once upon a time, people thought that the world was flat. This stopped them from going on what would have been an amazing adventure and remained where they are because they were caged by this 'reality'. But when some brave scientists were able to disprove this theory, mankind was set free to explore the ends of the earth. Emotional triggers might be based on myths that you have fed yourself and so every time you are confronted by a situation that triggers those emotions, you are trapped in what you feel. Break the cycle by disproving those myths.

The outcome may not be something that you like but whatever it is, you get to own your truth.

5. Embrace all of your peculiarities

Life is a fiery bouncy ball of unexpected twists and turns and it could hit us at any time. The people in our lives would come and go. You can't cling on to a memory or a person because you are afraid of what would happen to you after you let them go. This fear is mostly because you haven't come to a place of acceptance. You are unusual, you are unique and the experiences you have are crazy but that is what makes you exceptional. In embracing yourself, lean towards loving yourself more. When you love yourself, every other thing that happens to you is just secondary.

Powerful Techniques for Healing and Self-Protection

The default setting of any person when they feel threatened is to go to a place where they feel safe. You may not always have the luxury of running to your safe space. So, what do you do then? Stop. Take time out and chill. These powerful techniques I have learned have become a coping mechanism for me and I cannot remember a point in my life when I have been happier.

Affirmations

We are made up of the words that we speak to ourselves. If you do not speak to yourself, the words that other people speak to you would become the foundation on which your life is built. And we know that the world can be a cruel place. Some of the negative things that people say to you do not come from a place of malice. They just don't know any better. But regardless of the intentions behind their words, you do not want to leave your peace and sanity to the words of people. Affirmations are words that you speak to charge up your energy and sometimes cancel out the negatives words that people speak towards you. I start my day with the following chant;

"I am a strong powerful component in the universe and I have been empowered to take charge of my day"

Find phrases and positive words that you connect with. Whenever you are feeling overwhelmed by your emotions or the activities going on around you, speak those words and absorb the energy that they give out to you.

Bring Joy into your life

If you have been waiting for that one person whose connection would bring joy into your life, you have been looking in the wrong place. The only person that you need to complete your life is you. You need to stop waiting for some other person's permission to be happy. This is something that you are going to have to deal with by yourself. Empaths are not fond of this truth but trust me, the moment you accept this, you would activate healing in you that is so profound. It would also protect you from falling for just anyone who pops up on your radar. Start doing the things that you love, plan that dream vacation, take that cooking class. Life is too beautiful to spend it waiting. Live your best life now.

Connect with nature

I don't think that there are a lot of things as refreshing as connecting with nature. It revitalizes your soul and leaves you feeling uplifted. A simple walk in the woods can leave you mentally destressed. Surrounding yourself by nature is like entombing yourself in mother earth. This is symbolic of being in the womb which is one of the safest places we have ever known. When you are there, absorb the tranquil energy from what you are surrounded by. If you find yourself by the beach, listen to the sounds of the waves crashing on the shore. Picture your fears and anxiety being broken apart by those waves and let relief wash over you. Accept the blessings and protection energies that you get and believe that you are loved and protected. You would experience a feeling of wholesomeness.

Determine your limits

Empaths struggle with a sense of lack of control. This is the cause of the emotional turmoil that they are always experiencing. It feels as though the world and the events around them happen without their consent. This leaves them in a state of pain, hurt and emotional trauma. To overcome this, it is important to remind yourself daily that everything and anything that happens to you happens with your permission. It is perfectly okay to say no. Put the 'no' out there and let that be your limit. When you feel tired and weary and don't want to go on in terms of dealing with people and their drama, it is okay to say no. Don't let your fear of other people's perception control your reaction. Put your feet down and say no more than you normally would. The essence of this exercise is to empower you and get you to that place where you can embrace the control you have over your life.

Positive Affirmations All Empaths Must Know

With each chapter and segment of this book, I am sure that you got a more intimate knowledge of yourself. Now with that knowledge comes the need to take action. You know what they say, knowledge without action is useless. But before we get to the part where you start acting out the information and wisdom you have received, let us begin that journey by empowering the beautiful person within you. I talked about affirmations before and now we're going to get practical with them. Here are a few affirmations that I feel would be very impactful in the life of an empath

1. I am a beautiful and sensitive soul. My sensitivity is a powerful strength and with this strength, I change my world.

2. I am a very important person, and, in my life, I promise to have people value me as a person. My inner circle is made up of people who value my opinions, my presence, and my feelings.

3. Today I attract blessings and positive energies my way. I reject anything that would infect my world with negativity. My life is beautiful. My experiences are beautiful. My love is beautiful.

4. I have been blessed with the gift to intuitively recognize what is good for me. I listen to my instincts. I trust my instinct and I am protected by my instincts. As long as I listen to my inner voice, I will not come to harm.

5. Today I build a wall around me that protects my energy from people who are emotionally exhausting. I commit myself to staying in relationships that nurture me just as much as I nurture them.

6. I deserve happiness and so today, I will pamper myself. I will treat myself to a healthy diet. I will exercise my mind and body. Today, I am making a commitment to be good to myself.

Chapter Seven - The Healthy, Happy Empath

Now that we have looked at the injured empath as well as the problems that empaths face and then we've gone through this process where we find healing within, how do we know that we have been healed? That is the essence of this chapter. I want us to take a good look at what a happy empath looks like. Because yes, it is possible to be happy and healthy both emotionally and physically. It is always going to take a lot of work. There is no need to hide from that fact. We know that we are built differently than the average person and so the way we react to situations and events in our life is different. Despite the hurdles brought on by our inherent nature, we will find healing. There is no doubt about it but sometimes, the best thing that can motivate you into taking the best course of action for you would be to get a clear vision of yourself. And that is where we are getting to in this chapter. I am not trying to paint a rosy picture. Just in case you haven't noticed, I started this chapter by reiterating some of the difficulties that I feel we would encounter on some level. That said, I think it is time to unveil the person you could become if you stick to the course. Continue in your affirmations and stay healthy both mentally and physically and the result would be rewarding.

The 5 Powerful Lessons Every Empath Must Learn

1. Saying no does not make you a horrible person

When you put an empath in a position with their supposed to say yes or no, instinctively they want to say yes. This is their nature and, in a world, where everything is perfect, this is the right attitude to have. Unfortunately, the world is anything but perfect and so saying yes, every single time you're asked only sets you up for a life of regret. As you evolve on your journey as an empath. This is one of the most critical lessons you would learn. Life does not end when you say no.

As a matter of fact, the opposite is what happens. Your life begins at the end of your no.

2. It is perfectly okay to put yourself first

The empath is generous to a fault. They put the feelings and emotions of others before their own. This nature is what endears them to people but at the same time, it is what destroys them from the inside. On this journey, if you are going to become a better version of yourself, one lesson you must learn is that it is perfectly okay to put yourself first.

3. Your sensitivity is a strength

All your life, you have been told that emotions make a person weak. The fact that you have been sensitive to the things that happen around you has earned you the title of a weak and sensitive person but on this journey, you will discover that your sensitivity is one of your biggest strength. And the more information you acquire about yourself the more powerful you become.

4. You were never the problem

People are going to try and throw your nature in your face. Especially people with whom you have shared some kind of relationships with. Whether it's at work, in school or in your personal relationship. Because of their inability to understand the kind of person you are, it is always going to seem as though you are the problem from the onset. But with the information you get about yourself as you continue to study your personality and understand what empaths are about, you would realize that the problem was never you in the first place. And it is not about allocating the blame. It is about recognizing things for what they really are. Remind yourself constantly (no matter how loud they say otherwise) that the cause of the problem is not you for people's lack of understanding.

5. Happiness is a choice that you make

This here is not something that is unique to just empaths alone a lot of times we fail to realize that the way we feel is actually the only thing that we can control. And yet that is the very thing that we choose to leave in the hands of other people. Happiness is not going to come and knock on your door. It is not going to come in the form of a person who you assume is the perfect one for you. It is not going to be present even if you find that perfect relationship or you suddenly wake up wealthy. Happiness is like waking up every morning and deciding to brush your teeth. It is something that you have to strive for every day and if you take anything away from this particular section of the book, let it be the fact that you are in control of the state of your mind.

Daily Practices of a Healthy Empath

If happiness is something that you have to strive for every day, what then are those things that a happy empath would do to retain their happiness? It is a curious question especially when you consider the fact that happiness means a lot of things to different people. From my personal experience, true happiness does not come from the things that you can own or the things that you can buy. Genuine happiness is found in the little pleasures that you take in the little moments that come to you. It can be very fleeting which is why it is important to be present in every moment because if you miss out on those moments, you wouldn't miss opportunities to be happy. Many of us spend our days procrastinating are happiness. We think that if we are able to get that job if we are able to buy that house; if we finally get to meet that perfect person right now, our lives would be so much better and that is when we know we can finally find happiness. But the thing is that by declaring these words we deprive ourselves of a real shot at happiness. Stop waiting for happiness to happen to you. Use these daily exercises to inject some happiness into your life.

Take a minute to be grateful

One of the reasons that we are unable to find happiness is that we are so focused on the things that we don't have, that we forget about the things that we do have. We place so much value on what we hope to get and pay no attention to the blessings that are already in our lives. No matter how bad a situation is they are little blessings around it. And you can only find those blessings if you make a conscious effort. So, when you wake up in the morning take out a minute of your day to be thankful for all that you have. As they say, you have to develop an attitude of gratitude.

Begin your next adventure

When you get stuck in a rut, your life becomes a very boring place. You lose that sense of wonder which brings some kind of happiness to your life. It is hard to see the good things that you have and appreciate them for what they are and it's not necessarily because you are not thankful. I think it has more to do with the fact that you have lost the lust for life. Today, go on a mini-adventure. It doesn't have to be something grand. It could be something as simple as trying out a new cuisine or maybe starting a new sport. The goal is to bring a sense of newness into your life; to renew your passion for life. When you're passionate about your life, you find happiness in the littlest things.

Show yourself some love

You deserve happiness. I have said this several times and that goes to tell you how important it is. Now showing yourself love is something that many of us kick against instinctively because we think that it creates is a certain perception about us. The fact that we care so much about what other people may think about us more than what we think about ourselves says a lot about our mental state. You don't need to wait for people to love you. As a matter of fact, not many people can love you more than you love yourself. If you want to welcome love into your life, the first place to start from is with you. Show yourself some love. Be kinder to yourself, take out time to pamper yourself. I know they say that going out to eat alone may seem a little depressing.

Again, this is the perception of other people. If you want to dine out, I recommend doing it once in a month or so. Take yourself to the finest restaurant you can afford, treat yourself to a lovely meal. Or go to a spa if that is your thing. Enjoy a nice massage. These are little ways you can show yourself, love.

Take a moment to breath

We live very busy lives and the world we are in today moves at a very fast pace. So much so that from the moment you wake up, to the second you put your head down for the day, it seems as though 24 hours just flew by. It is important to take pauses throughout your day. You don't have to do anything significant during those pauses. Something as simple as just focusing on your breathing can do a lot to improve the outcome of your day. When you are feeling tense and wound up, put a pause on whatever it is you are doing. Take a deep breath and exhale; imagine that the tension and stress that you are feeling is flowing out with that breath. There are several breathing exercises that are designed specifically to reduce stress. You could look those up on the internet and maybe try it out. If that sounds a little too complicated for you, just stick to taking pauses during your day. Stop and smell the proverbial roses.

Have a Vision of your future

In very simple terms, this is called dreaming. When you stop dreaming, it is very easy to lose your happiness. That is not to say we should not be rooted in the moment. What I mean is that a vision of your future offers you an alternative that you can walk towards without detaching you from your present. It is important that you recognize the dynamics of this. Going forward, I urge you to dream a little more than you normally would. Picture the happiness that this vision gives you and let it empower your present.

Stop Empathizing with Pain and Start Empathizing with Joy

As empaths, we have a tendency to connect ourselves with pain. When we see someone in pain, we reflect that pain in our lives. This causes us to go through that pain as if it were our own pain. But when it comes to joy or other positive emotions, for some reason we have a detachment. We are unable to reflect that joy and in so doing, we don't live through that joy as if it were our own. Our bias toward pain is not something that is easily understood. Perhaps it is because the pain has an intensity that calls us or maybe the fact that we can be actively involved in resolving some other person's pain. When it comes to joy, on the other hand, it feels as though because there is nothing we can do about it, we don't get involved as much and I think that this is the crux of the problem. When we witness emotions in other people, we are psychologically programmed to react to it and not just react. We want to do something about it.

Well, that was just me speculating, however, science tells us something similar. According to science, our brains do not react with the same intensity to joy as it does to pain. What that means is that as humans, we have an easier time sharing in the pain and suffering of others then we do in sharing their joy. I believe that this experience is even more true for empaths. Experts believe that there is a lot more psychological reward when you are reacting to other people's pain than there is when you react to their joy. This goes on to reinforce my theory that we feel a lot better when we are involved in someone's process and pain allows you more involvement than joy does. When you see a person experiencing joy, you simply have to be happy for that person. But when he comes to pain, our "fixer personality' is put to good use. Now, this does not mean that we want people to be in pain all the time or even at all. It just goes to show what we do subconsciously.

And just because you are programmed to do something subconsciously doesn't mean that your personality has been defined by this. You can take the step to change this attitude. It is good to respond to the pain in other people, but it is also good to respond to their happiness. This is not just for the person you are reacting to but for yourself as well. In order to be a happy, healthy and well-grounded empath, it is important that you strike a balance between these two reactions. When you see someone happy, go ahead and actively rejoice with them. There is no rule that says you cannot do something to celebrate that happiness. If you make the conscious effort to celebrate the happiness of others you would find that there are also rewards involved in this too.

So, today I want you to add to your list of affirmations the desire to celebrate the happiness of other people. When next someone in your circle announces a piece of good news, offer to take them out to celebrate the event. You don't even need to wait until something positive happens. You can just whip out a pen and paper and draft an appreciation letter to your friend, family or loved one the old-fashioned way. Think of a creative way to showcase your empathy for their happiness. It may be a bit of a drag in the beginning, but as you keep at it, it becomes a normal part of you.

Practice Non-Reactive Empathy

Telling an empath to stop reacting to the emotions and energies that they get off other people is like telling them to stop breathing. This is who we are and by now, I am hoping that you have come to that place of acceptance. Now, this segment is about getting you to that place where you don't react to every energy or vibe around you. This can be difficult especially if you're surrounded by people in pain. However, you must bear in mind that to become a happy and healthy empath, this is a skill you are going to have to learn. Look at the things going on around you and develop a different way of reacting to those things. See how I am not telling you to stop reacting? I'm simply saying develop a different form of reaction. To be able to do this, you have to come from a place of self-awareness. Knowing who you are and how certain things make you feel equip you to be more prepared as you can anticipate your reaction.

Another thing you have to understand is that nothing is the way it seems. You may have emotionally walked through that person's shoes but that doesn't mean you have a full picture of what is going on. You see, this is a common mistake that is very peculiar to us as empaths. We feel that our connection to the experience of people gives us access to the whole picture. Let us say, for instance, you stumble across a homeless man on the street. He is holding out his tin cup as usual and asking for any spare change. You immediately react emotionally to his present circumstance and you know how he feels in that moment. But the thing is you only about that specific moment. Bearing this in mind would make it easier for you to develop a different reaction or in the very least reduce your emotional reaction to things.

Scientists tell us that 90% of what we do is based on habit. Therefore, if you want to learn how to develop new ways of doing things, you would have to retrain your brain. To be less reactive, I urge you to consciously take a pause before you react. That pause could make a difference between overreacting and reacting appropriately. One neat trick I had was to pinch myself every time I feel like my emotions are going on overdrive. It acts as a warning signal reminding me to slow down. It took a while for me to get this message but today, I am better for it. I still get affected by the pain that other people feel but I won't dive into everything emotion's first anymore. I feel, I think and then I react.

Chapter Eight - Empathy as a Superpower

Now that we have taken off our rose-tinted glasses, we can see empathy for what it really is. And despite all the challenges and struggles that we go through as empaths, it is safe to say that empathy is a superpower. Empathy is that defining quality that makes us human. The ability to see our fellow human go through life's journey; whether good or bad and have their experiences reflected in our own lives without us having to actually go through those experiences is incredible. As empaths, we set the pace for humanity. We are more than observers in the world's bibliography of anything to do with human experiences. We are participators and, in a way, I would say we are the bookkeepers. It is a cool thing when you think about it. To be that person who witnesses life from the view of the other person. I don't care what people say. They may say that you are too emotional or too reactional or just crazy. We are proud empaths and there is no better time than right now to own the power that comes with the name.

The 7 Natural Gifts that All Empaths Possess

1. Empaths are very creative: The unique perspective given to empaths allow them to see the world in the way that most people don't. This view opens us up to a different dimension of things. In other words, we approach situations from a different angle giving us the unique ability to come up with creative solutions. And even when we are not coming up with innovative solutions, we are very adept at creating exceptional art.

2. Empaths are natural healers: Our connection to the things around us whether people, plants or animals give us a link that makes us natural healers. We have an instinctive understanding of the life energy that flows around us, and we play on this knowledge to provide assistance

to whoever and whatever needs it. Combine this with our biological need to provide care and you have the perfect natural healer.

3. Empaths are alert to dangers in the environment: Thanks again to our connection to the world around us when we enter a room, there something in our subconscious or our being that alerts us immediately we get a sense that there is a threat to our lives in that space. This is not something you can explain. It just happens and it is one of those gifts that we are thankful for.

4. Empaths can spot a lie a mile away: This has got to be my favorite gift as an empath; the ability to spot a lie. It doesn't matter how well-crafted the lie is or how much physical evidence is available to support the lie, the moment an empath encounters a lie, they sense its falseness.

5. Empaths can spot the truth: The same way an empath can spot a lie is the same way they can detect the truth. In our dealings with people, we find them doing their best to mask their true intentions or their true feelings. Our connection to people and our ability to read their energy allows see beneath those layers of pretense and unveil the truth.

6. Empaths get the best experiences: Imagine being able to experience the kaleidoscope of human emotion? That plane of intensity leaves you with a variety of experiences is that not many people would ever have the privilege to experience. The moment we are able to get our feelings under control, we open up the doors to experience life at its best.

7. Empaths are good at reading body language: Communication can either be verbal or nonverbal. Most people are only able to understand communication at a verbal level and even then, their inability to sense the true intentions of people makes it difficult to truly understand the direction of that communication. For empaths, this is hardly a problem. To add to that, they can read the body language of a person to determine what they mean or how they feel

The Best Jobs for Empaths

In my experience, empaths who are self-aware can walk in any field that they put their mind to. It is those who are still struggling with their gifts that find it difficult to function maximally in certain areas. And even then, I feel that this has more to do with their individual personality than their gifts as empaths. Now it is one thing to work in a certain field and it is another thing to thrive in that particular field. For this segment, I am going to focus on career pathways where empath is more likely to utilize their gifts and be successful.

This list is more of a guide so, be careful when applying it to your life. You have to factor in things like your area of specialization, your basic skill sets as well as your talents. Deciding to take a detour into these fields based on your gift as an empath alone is not going to guarantee you the kind of success you desire. The message behind everything I am saying that being an empath would complement the skill sets as well as any other basic requirements for these job roles in their respective industries. With that out of the way, let us explore those job roles.

Psychologist: The empaths ability to listen is one of the things that qualify them for this job. However, it would require an empath who is self-aware to thrive as a psychologist. The reason for this is that empaths in their raw and untrained state tend to react emotionally. Psychologists need a sense of detachment. Even if they can identify with the feelings and emotions that their patient is going through, there still has to be that line for them to be able to offer an objective perspective and as well as creative solutions. Nevertheless, I believe that an empath was born for this job.

Veterinarian: In almost every setting, your local vet is also known as the animal whisperer. They have a way of connecting with the animals under their care and this is not a skill that is learned in any classroom. It is something that is inborn. You need the training in order to provide the right solution, but you need that intuitive ability in order to truly understand the problem.

Artist: It is common knowledge that artists are people with extremely tortured souls and that's because they seem to be sensitive to the world around them. It would make sense to come to this conclusion because it would require you to have a great depth of insight to be able to see things that other people look at as ordinary and transform it into something spectacular. Artists are the reason you can look at a painting and be moved to tears. Or you can listen to a sound and be transported to another universe or you read a set of words and your emotions are stirred. This comes from empathy

Guidance Counselor: This is similar to the psychologist, except this time around, you are helping young people determine their career path and helping kids make the right choices in school. And I feel like this is a role that is very suited to an empath because they can relate to these people like no other person can and also, their intuitive ability to read the true emotions and intentions of people put them in a better position to offer advice when it comes to things like their career or sexual the choices in school among other things.

Lawyer: People without voices need an advocate to speak for them and no person can do this better than someone who is an empath the ability to relate with the situation and the astuteness provided by their training would make them a lethal combination in the courtroom.

How Empaths Can Use Their Gifts to Manifest Success

Empaths are in possession of a lot of gifts that I fell would give them a head start in the workplace their success is not only linked to their career. If applied correctly different areas of your life, you would find yourself thriving. For this segment, I am going to look at five different areas in your life and we would look at how you can use your gift as an empath to get a "leg-up" in that department.

In your career

Empath Survival Guide

Regardless of the kind of job that you do, the odds are, you have other people that you work with. For an empath, this gives you the extra advantage because you have an innate understanding of how the relationship dynamics between people work. For you to succeed in the workplace; here is how to work your gifts to your advantage;

1. Use your gift of insight into problems to develop innovative solutions. Your challenge in this regard would be getting your voice heard. Relax, speak your truth and impress your colleagues with your amazing ideas.
2. Use your ability to sense energy to work on timing. This is very helpful when pitching new projects to the boss or lodging a complaint.

In your relationships

For the empath who is yet to understand their personality, their relationships are either complicated or one-sided. With the knowledge you have gained, you can build relationships that are healthy and thrive.

1. Use your gift of separating the truths from the lie, you can actively select the kind of people who you instinctively know to have your best interest at heart. This keeps the energy around you positive
2. Use your creative ability to come up with gift ideas, fun activities and other unique experiences that bond people together and foster friendships

In your finances

Money is tricky for anyone. Empath or not you need basic financial knowledge in order to effectively manage your money. Understandably, money is not a strong motivating force for the empath but there is no reason why you cannot be wealthy. That said, your empathic abilities can help you in the following areas;

1. Monetize your passion. Empaths are moved by the things that they are passionate about. If you can find a way to make your passion a source of income, you would hit a jackpot.
2. Use your network to build net worth. Your relationships are usually your most valuable assets. Grow that and your assets grow.

In your mental health

As much as empaths deal with a lot of emotional problems, if they can also have the best emotional experience. To thrive mentally, do the following;

1. Use your energy radar to filter the kinds of energy you allow into your space. With positive energies, you grow. Negative energies, on the other hand, have a withering effect on you.
2. Use your ability to connect to establish a connection with your true intentions. People walk through life confused about the things that they want. This puts them in a terrible mental state. But not you. Put your mind to it and you can at every point in time know exactly what you want.

In your spiritual life

Your spirituality is not about religion now. But about having harmony in body, mind, and spirit. Empaths are one of the most spiritual beings and you can amplify the experience by doing any of the following

1. Tap into the energy that surrounds nature to revitalize and refresh yourself. This would drain out any of the negative excesses brought into your life and help keep you in a state of bliss
2. Plug your natural talent into your gift of perception. This way, you are connected to a seemingly endless supply of ideas. People tend to burn out and when they do, they become restless in their quest to regain what they have lost. Your empathic gift can provide a sustainable supply for your talent

The Power of Empathy in the Modern Day

The world that we live in today is chaotic. There is hardly any day that you turn on the news and you would not witness the misery and tragedy that other people are dealing with. The advent of technology has made it possible for media to get to the farthest corners of the earth and bring these tales of woes to your doorstep. With constant exposure to these things, it is not surprising that people have become emotionally detached from the sufferings of people. It has gotten so bad that empathy has become an almost extinct commodity in the human range of emotions.

Today's world is evolving and it is my opinion that without empathy, the world would topple into a chaotic state. Empathy is what creates a balance between the pain that one human is capable of inflicting and the joy that another human is capable of giving. Empathy is what characterizes humanity. We have our differences in experiences, in personalities and in our beliefs. Empathy is the bridge that connects us all. They say that love is a general language and everyone understands it. This was perhaps true a few centuries ago. In the state where the world is right now, love has multiple languages and it takes a level of self-awareness to not just speak it but to speak it fluently.

Empathy is the new universal language. The ability to connect with another being and be interested in their welfare enough to invest in it is what the world needs and this is empathy at the general level. Empathy responds to need and the world is a place that is full of needy people and I don't mean that in the 'clingy' sense. Everyone needs to be heard on some level by someone else. Without empathy, that need would continue to grow for a long time leading to tensions. Today's world is running on the fumes created by these tensions and empathy is the only way to diffuse the situation.

All I am trying to say here is that you are valuable now more than ever. We started this journey with people's perception of empaths. And in retrospect, it would be safe to say that their analogy puts empaths somewhere between an alien and a crazy person. I believe that now you know better. Now you know that you are a sensitive, spiritual being that is full of light and life. The struggles that you have had up to this point are temporary and if you consistently put in the knowledge you have gained here to work, you have the potential to be an extraordinary person. You are the superhero that the world needs in their corner. Your presence is a constant reminder that there is a lot of good in the world and we do not have to look to the skies for angels.

Conclusion

At the start of the book, my goal was to document my journey from being a crazy, out of control empath to this person who is self-aware and rooted in the gifts that I have been given. But with each paragraph, I started picturing your face. As the features of your face became clearer, I started seeing your personality and from your personality, you became a whole person to me. Somewhere along the way, this stopped being my journey. It became our journey and it made me even more excited to share everything that I have learned on my way here with you. People have tried to define us by their own experiences and for the longest time, this has been the yardstick for empaths. We are sensitive, we are emotional, we don't have it together and if like me you imbibed that message, I can imagine how troubled your life must have been up to this point. And this is why I wrote this book. I wanted to reflect the potential that every empath has. We are not reclusive, cry babies but powerful warriors with the ability to change our world. Try that on for size!

We took a lot of detours on this journey and the purpose of it was to look into every aspect of our day to day living. I wanted to break it down into relatable bits. I see this book as a mirror and the clearer it is, the better the vision of yourself that you get. We started off by changing the narrative on who we are and then gradually went into how we deal with everyday situations. We even walked into the dark side of being an empath and to be honest, that was a very difficult process for me. I saw some of the mistakes I have made and that brought back memories of some of the lowest points in my life. I got a very distinct feeling that you had lived through similar pains too. But the good things is that starring into that abyss empowered my decision to be better. Which is why when we moved to the chapters where we talked about our unique abilities. The most intriguing bit for me is the discovery that I actually have the ability to define my life. And this is something that we all share as humans, more so for empaths.

I am hoping that after everything you have read and discovered in this book, that you find the courage to embrace the strength that I know you have on the inside and that you start living your best life now. I can wish from now to the ends of the universe but it is not going to change a thing if you do not believe that you are deserving of this precious gift. Years ago, when I felt that my life was over and I had nothing else to offer, all I wanted was a second chance at life. I wanted a complete do-over. During the years it took me to learn everything I have unloaded in this book; I got my second chance. I just didn't know that 'this' was it. And by 'this', I am referring to the knowledge I had gained over time. My mother used to tell me that knowledge is useless until you put it to action and at first, that was what this information was for me. Until I started making it practical. And so, I am going to pass on that bit of elderly wisdom across to you. Take everything that you have gained from reading this book and apply it. It is in applying it that you would discover what works for you and what doesn't. As you sieve through that process, you become better, wiser and stronger.

This book outlines the process of getting you to a happier and healthier place step by step. I ensured that content is positive, relatable and practical. Being an empath is not an alien concept. This is our reality and part of my objective was to write a book with a balanced perspective on every aspect of our lives. If I wanted to be dramatic, I would say that this book was about tipping the odds in your favor and I believe that we were able to achieve this. In your hands right now a tool that shows your strengths and weaknesses. It highlights your interests and your passions and it clearly outlines your risks and your rewards. It is not a magician's wand that you can simply flick your wrists, say the magic word and transform your life overnight but it puts the power of transformation in your hands.

And now that we have come to the end, it is my earnest desire that your process does not end the second that you close this book. I want the words that are contained in this book to come alive in your heart. I want them to inspire you in moments when you feel down and activate a passion in you that sees you pursuing your dreams to the fullest. However, as an empath, I understand what your biggest struggle in all of this is going to be and with that knowledge, here is my wish for you. I wish that you would see yourself for the wonderful person that you are and ultimately accept this gift that has been given to you. I can almost see the gears in your brain working in unison and I hope that they steer you towards that space where you can finally accept that you are deserving of happiness. That you no longer need to keep putting your needs and your dreams on the back burner for everyone else. You have just as much right as everyone else to be happy. That is not to say that I want you to stop being you…just a friendly reminder that your dreams and aspirations are a part of who you are. On that note, I say welcome to the best days of the rest of your life. Keep being authentic.

NARCISSISTIC RELATIONSHIP

Discover How to Recover, Protect and Heal Yourself After a Toxic Abusive Relationship with a Narcissist

Table of Contents

Introduction **95**

Chapter 1 - Unraveling Narcissism **101**
    The 7 Warning Signs of Narcissistic Personality Disorder 101
    What Causes Narcissism? 107
    4 Types of Narcissists You Need to Stay Away From 109
    The 4 Types of People That Narcissists Are Attracted to 110

Chapter 2 - Staying One Step Ahead **113**
    11 Ways to Know You're in a Relationship with a Narcissist 113
    Dangerous Manipulation Tactics Used by Narcissists 120
    5 Things Every Narcissist Likes to Say 126
    5 Triggers for Narcissistic Rage 128

Chapter 3 - When Enough Is Enough **133**
    5 Essential Tips for Dealing with a Narcissist the Right Way 133
    5 Phrases to Instantly Disarm a Narcissist 138

Chapter 4 - Cutting the Cord **142**
    Why It's So Hard to Break up with a Narcissist 142
    The 7 Stages of Trauma Bonding 144
    How to Break Up With a Narcissist for Good 145
    Using the Gray Rock Method to Your Advantage 148

Chapter 5 - Healing From Narcissistic Abuse **151**
    The 5 Stages of Recovery from Narcissistic Abuse 152
    5 Transformative Truths Every Victim Must Face 156
    Essential Exercises to Strengthen the Healing Heart & Mind 160
    Life-Altering Affirmations to Heal Past Hurts 162

Chapter 6 - Breaking the Cycle **167**
    6 Reasons Why You Keep Attracting Narcissists 167
    7 Ways to Spot a Narcissist on the First Date 170
    4 Ways to Stop Attracting Narcissists Once and for All 175
    9 Powerful Tips for Developing Unbreakable Self-Love 177

Chapter 7 - Loving Again **181**
    7 Mistakes to Avoid When You Start Dating Again 181

5 Early Signs You've Finally Found a Good Partner 185
8 Great Habits to Start Your New Relationship the Right Way 189

Conclusion 193

Introduction

If you've picked up this book, you may be wondering if you're in a relationship with a narcissist. Alternatively, you may know you're in a relationship with a narcissist and are now wondering how to get out of it. Or you might be trying to assess if you really need to get out or if things will get better.

Our you may have come to this book because you have come out of a relationship that started off well but then left you so bruised and unsure of what went wrong that you are now looking for ways to heal and move on. You want to avoid a repeat of the devastation that a narcissist can wreak on your wellbeing.

Some of you may even be in a new relationship with someone who was hurt by a narcissist and wants to know how to help them move forward.

Whatever brought you here, you've come to the right place. In the chapters that follow, you'll learn how to identify narcissistic abuse and how to spot a narcissist, so you don't get stung again. You'll learn what they say, what they do, and how they react.

You'll learn how to protect yourself and use techniques to back away so that you don't attract the rage of this particularly difficult personality type. Most importantly, you'll be given the tools to help you recover from your experience and move on with your life to a happier future and better relationships.

Narcissistic Relationship

As someone who has come across a few narcissists in my time, I have closely studied this troubling personality type and unlocked many of the secrets that make them who they are. Once you truly understand them, they lose their hold over you and reveal themselves for what they are — troubled and deeply lonely individuals who are sadly too damaged to enjoy healthy, balanced relationships with others. *You can't help them.*

Read this book, and you'll come away not only with greater understanding but also the tools to free yourself of the narcissist in your life. You can look forward to greater peace and security in your future relationships, a sense of safety and wellbeing, and greater self-confidence — something that a narcissist is quite skilled at undermining.

Here's what we'll cover:

- **How to spot a narcissist**

You'll find out what they'll say to you, how they will get under your skin and, most importantly, how they'll make you feel. We'll look at the different types of narcissists and some examples of how they tend to behave in certain situations, for example, on a first date.

We'll also look at what makes someone into a narcissist, and who they really are under that tough exterior (clue: very immature). Knowing just how small and frightened these people are beneath that smooth surface is key to understanding their behavior and to no longer being affected by it.

- **How to recover from narcissistic abuse**

A narcissist can do damage seemingly without regret. With their words and their behavior, they can have you doubting yourself, feeling unsure of your sanity, and living in a state of siege. They thrive on drama, discord, and conflict, while the people around them struggle to do anything apart from ward off their next attack. But you can break this cycle and not fall into it again.

In this book, you'll find out how to empower yourself, heal, and restore your sense of self-worth after narcissistic abuse. We'll also look at how to safely break up, disengage or move on from a narcissist without attracting their narcissistic rage.

- **How to deal with a narcissist in the moment**

Unfortunately, this personality trait is reasonably common. In fact, there are times when it's easier to simply get along with a narcissist. One example is when you have one at your workplace and you otherwise love your job. Another is when you have a narcissistic family member who you have to maintain some contact with for the sake of the wider peace. Why should you leave to escape just this one person?

The answer is, you don't. But what you do need are some simple techniques to prepare for those encounters. This way, you can deal with the narcissist in a calm, assertive manner "in the moment" when they attempt to push your buttons. The other benefit of this is that they are likely to get bored, move on to their next victim, and leave you alone.

- **How to escape from a narcissist**

One thing that narcissists cannot tolerate is being ignored or abandoned. This triggers all of their buried feelings, often buried from childhood, that led them to behave abusively in the first place. You can be certain that they will make leaving as difficult for you as it is for them. Once you have escaped, the narcissist in your life will simply move on to someone else — but before that happens, you can expect an escalation of all of their worst behaviors. In the most serious cases, you may be in actual danger.

However, there are ways to disarm the narcissist, back away slowly, and protect yourself. These can be learned. Most importantly, these techniques will make the process easier and less distressing for you. With some planning and easy-to-access tactics under your belt, you'll soon be looking forward to a more peaceful future, far away from this damaged and damaging individual.

- **How to help other victims of narcissistic abuse**

Dealing with a narcissist can leave you feeling isolated and unsure of your own sanity. Read on for essential tools that will help you not only recover yourself, but also spot the signs in other victims and help them to break free, too. As more is known of this personality type, I hope to see a world where they don't get away with it nearly as much as they seem to right now. Narcissists thrive on secrecy, and by writing this book and exposing their secrets, I hope you will learn from my work and come away feeling better equipped to simply disengage from them.

Through my writing, research, and close study of this particular personality type, I have helped many people escape from narcissistic abuse. Being caught in a relationship with a narcissist is something that I liken to the "frog in the pan of water" analogy — by the time the frog realizes the water is boiling, it's too late to jump out.

With a narcissist, you find yourself struggling to escape, worn out from their mind games, tantrums, and cutting insults. You end up doubting yourself. You may feel that you are enmeshed in a seemingly endless situation and no longer have the courage to escape.

Don't let that happen to you! Educate yourself, learn the signs to look for, and how to look after yourself and others. A narcissist has the power to cause great damage and untold hurt to those around them, but it doesn't have to be that way. They are only as strong as you allow them to be.

When you truly understand this personality type, you will see that they are not nearly as powerful as they appear. You will know exactly what to say and exactly how to behave so that they simply get bored and move on to someone else. In my experience, narcissists are very difficult, if not impossible, to treat.

They don't change, and they don't seek help. Often, they are perfectly content with the status quo and resistant to any change or greater equality in their relationships with others. Why would they want change when they have everyone dancing around them?

So, as hard as it is, there's no point wishing for them to change, either, despite what they may promise you at times. They will never change. All you can do is accept that and try to move on with your own life.

With my help, you can look forward to a happier future. You can escape. You can have a life free of drama and the toxic influence of a narcissist. You can feel greater contentment and a sense of safety and purpose. More importantly, you deserve to. Narcissists are very good at playing on our better selves, on manipulating the kindest and most empathetic people to meet their own selfish needs. You don't have to fall victim to this, and you don't have to get drawn into their games.

Read on to find out how.

Chapter 1 - Unraveling Narcissism

In this chapter, we start to unravel narcissism to find out what it is, what causes it, and how to spot it in others. We also look at the kinds of people that tend to fall prey to the wiles of a narcissist.

We'll give you some clues to look out for when meeting people for the first time, and odd behaviors to look out for. Let's go!

The 7 Warning Signs of Narcissistic Personality Disorder

Narcissism is a recognized personality disorder that is thought to affect around 6% of the population, though many who suffer from it may be undiagnosed. It's characterized by a grandiose sense of self (often very much undeserved), a ruthless need to exploit others, and a strong sense of entitlement. Narcissists are also prone to narcissistic rages. Unfortunately, they keep their true selves hidden and can also be extremely charming when they need to be.

Once you know what to look for, narcissists are generally easy to spot, and you can keep them at a distance without being drawn into their world. But what are you looking for?

Read on for the 7 key signs of Narcissistic Personality Disorder if you think someone you know or are close to may have it. See if any of it rings true for you.

1. **They have a grandiose sense of self**

Narcissistic Relationship

The narcissist always has to be the best: the best looking, the most successful, the most interesting. While this can be charming or endearing in the short term, it quickly becomes wearing for those around this person, as they struggle to have their own achievements and needs recognized.

Narcissists believe that they are special and unique. They believe that they should only associate with other special people and that they deserve the best possible treatment and attention in any situation. They train others to believe this too, so that before you know it, you're dancing around this person and treating them with excessive care, often at a considerable cost to your own time, wellbeing, energy and personal growth.

They will also exaggerate and lie about their achievements, and downplay, ignore or refuse to acknowledge those of others. Whatever you may have achieved in your life, you can be certain that the narcissist has done it too — and done it better.

Classic narcissist behavior:

You: Oh, guess what? My novel is being published!

Them: That's nice. That reminds me, I'm going to write a novel. I love writing, and I was always very good at English. Everyone always told me I should write a book. Who is your agent, and can you send me their details? I would like to talk to them about my planned book.

2.   They live in a fantasy world

In their own world, they are successful, wonderful, and there to be admired. If you support and reflect these beliefs back at them, you will enjoy their approval. If, however, you dare to challenge them on the truth or details of their many achievements, be prepared for a serious backlash. You'll soon learn to tread carefully around the narcissist to avoid any repercussions or **narcissistic rage**, which knows few boundaries.

Classic narcissist behavior

If a narcissist visits your home, expect to feed them, wait on them, and clean up after them, and possibly lend them money, without any reciprocation of the favor. If you visit them, expect to be given little to eat and to simply listen to them talk about themselves. After all, you are lucky to be around them.

3. They require lavish praise and undivided attention

If you're in the company of a narcissist, after a while you'll start to notice something: it's all one way. You are simply there to listen to them talk about how wonderful, talented, how special they are. They want you to hear how many friends they have and how successful they are in their career.

Try and get something back from them or ask them to recognize you in any way and prepare to be frustrated: the narcissist is simply unable to pay attention to anyone else. It goes against their belief that they are the one who must be looked after, deferred to, and fussed over. They find it incredibly difficult to focus on or recognize others.

Classic narcissist behavior

You are at a party, celebrating the pregnancy of a friend. The narcissist will use the opportunity to announce their own plans to have a baby and somehow you'll end up drinking champagne and congratulating them, while they stand in the middle of the circle, smiling and enjoying the attention. Meanwhile, the pregnant friend is forgotten.

4. They have an extreme sense of entitlement

Of course, we all deserve to be treated with respect and kindness, but a narcissist takes this to another level. You may be groomed over time to accept their demands if you know them personally and accept that it's "just the way they are," but it's often jaw-dropping to see their sense of entitlement play out with other people.

Often, seeing a narcissist out in the world is a lightbulb moment for their victims. You may also see the most entitled behavior in how they treat others and feel embarrassed for them. You would be quite amazed at their ability to make the most outrageous demands, seemingly for the fun of it.

How do they treat waiters, reception staff, shopkeepers? They may be overly warm to those that treat them with deference, but watch out if someone dares to put them in their place or refuses to assist them with their often unreasonable demands.

Classic narcissist behavior

You're in a foreign city and looking for a bank. The narcissist will walk into a nearby hotel and demand that the receptionist looks up the directions of a bank, writes it down for them, and then — as an afterthought — gives them detailed instructions on various local museums. If the receptionist refuses to help them, they will feel extremely angry and become rude and petulant, and complain bitterly about how unreasonable the person was.

5.   They exploit others without guilt or shame

We are all guilty at times of overstepping the mark with others, and for most people, once we realize this we apologize and make amends. We may feel shame or guilt and vow to learn from our mistake and do better next time.

Narcissistic Relationship

But for the narcissist, there is no sense of guilt or shame. There is only rage and a sense of fierce injustice if they get called out for their behavior — after all, they are *special*. They are allowed to break the rules. Unlike normal people, the narcissist is constantly looking for a way in — and they are very good at playing on people's natural courtesy and generosity to meet their own needs.

Narcissists don't see any point in helping others for its own sake. All they care about is getting their own needs met, and they are prepared to behave as badly as they need to for this to happen. The only thing that may stop them is the worry that they are going to go too far and lose access to the person or thing they are exploiting: then, and only then, will they pull back temporarily so that they can continue to use and abuse in future.

Classic narcissist behavior

A narcissist will accept your offer to go out for the day, but will "forget" their wallet. You'll end up paying for their lunch, drinks, and entry fees. At the last moment, though, in a shop, they will suddenly "find" their wallet and buy themselves a new bag with all the money you've saved them. On the train home, they will mention that they'll pay you back, but you'll never see that money again, or even get a thank-you for treating them all day.

Or let's say you meet someone at a party who is a friend of a friend. They shower you with attention and through your friend, track down your email or phone number. Before you know it, they are passing through your town — because you had such a great chat at the party, is it OK if they stop by your house, around lunchtime? Before you know it, you're feeding them lunch and listening to them talk about themselves for two hours, lending them a book and helping them solve a problem with their phone — all on your day off.

6. They bully, belittle, and humiliate

To control others, you need to keep them feeling small and weak, and no one is better at this than a narcissist. They are experts at hunting down your weak points or sensitivities and then using this knowledge to bully and humiliate you whenever you seem to be getting ahead of yourself. To them, it's all a game. They like making others feel small because it makes them feel powerful, and it suits them to do this to those close to them because it makes them easier to control.

Classic narcissist behavior

You're dressed up and feeling good about yourself, and the narcissist will make a snide comment about your appearance, laugh at you, or simply refuse to acknowledge the effort you've gone to. If you appear too confident, they will come out with a nasty comment about your hair or your clothes to take you down a peg.

7. They have no empathy

This is perhaps the most chilling characteristic of a narcissist, as well as their central trait. They lack basic empathy and simply can not relate to the pain of others in any meaningful way. They may be able to fake it, but really, they feel nothing for the suffering of others. Some of the more malignant narcissists (more on this later) even seem to get some strange joy out of watching those around them suffer.

Classic narcissist behavior

You've just broken up with your boyfriend. You share the details with the narcissist and get no sympathy or comfort in return, just a bored comment about how the relationship was dragging on anyway and how you seem to always be so unlucky in love. They change the subject to talk about how well their own relationship is going.

What Causes Narcissism?

Narcissism is believed by many psychologists to have its roots in childhood. Often, it appears linked to a combination of both smothering a child with love and approval, and also neglecting them. Narcissists may have been sent to boarding school, for example, so they had holidays of luxury and privilege interspersed with long periods of institutional care where they felt alone and abandoned by their parents.

Small children tend to be quite selfish and lacking in empathy, as these are traits that diminish with maturity. The narcissist, however, never seems to learn to be kinder. They may have been overindulged as a child and allowed to get away with murder, yet also neglected by their main caregivers, never learning to feel empathy or think about the impact of their behavior on others.

Sometimes they have something happen to them that is so traumatic that they remain stuck in a selfish, immature way of dealing with others. Grown-up, but behaving like a baby. Again, this may be down to their caregivers not giving them the tools to treat others well.

As with all personality traits, it's impossible to say just how much can be put down to childhood experiences and how much is simply temperament and genes. What matters for those around the narcissist is how to deal with him or her, not what caused them to be the way they are.

It's important to remember, however, that the childhood roots of narcissism mean that it's very much a fundamental aspect of this person's nature, not something they can change, and not in any way your fault. You will find it very difficult, if not impossible, to change a narcissist. All you can do is change the way you react to them.

When is it narcissism and when is it just confidence or arrogance?

It's estimated that around 6% of the adult population suffers from narcissism. But what makes it different from the arrogance we see in popular culture? What distinguishes narcissism from the selfie culture and the self-promotion and showing off we see on social media, for example?

The difference often comes down to how authentic this confidence is — if it's genuine, it tends not to cause problems. But if it's hiding a much more uncertain person, it can be a disaster. While there is nothing wrong with demonstrating self-confidence in your life, even if it sometimes tips over into arrogance, narcissism is something different. They suffer from jealousy and are chronic "bucket dippers" — always seeking to dip into someone else's bucket of self-esteem in a flawed attempt to fill their own.

The narcissist is totally lacking in any form of self-confidence — deep down, they are actually a very small, frightened child. Their grandiose behavior is defensive and a way of protecting themselves from further harm. What looks like entitled behavior is actually an act, concealing someone with very little self-worth.

This is not true self-confidence, which is a trait that generally makes people more pleasant to be around. You can also be an arrogant person at times but still be a loving partner, for example. A narcissist, on the other hand, has a personality disorder and it's difficult, if not impossible, to have a healthy and mutually satisfying relationship with them.

4 Types of Narcissists You Need to Stay Away From

Narcissists come in different forms, and some are easier to spot than others. All, however, are worth avoiding. Here are four recognizable types and what to look for in each:

1. Overt narcissists

They make life (relatively) easy in that you can spot them a mile off. These are the kinds of people you find bragging on Twitter about their latest achievement or lying about how much their car cost, or how much they earn.

Overt narcissists are also prone to public blowups and meltdowns, which again makes them easy to look out for and avoid. They can be very charming and seductive when they want something, but once they have it, they will move on.

2. Covert or closet narcissists

These guys are harder to spot and better at concealing their true natures. They may present themselves as saint-like, doing lots of work for charity and high-profile good deeds. Scratch that pristine surface, though, or get them on their own, and you'll find a narcissist.

3. Toxic narcissists

Narcissism, like all personality traits, exists on a spectrum. A little is healthy, a bit more annoying, but a lot — dangerous.

Toxic narcissists are at the more extreme end of the spectrum, so be prepared for drama if you let one of these into your life. They may be spiteful, extremely nasty or bullying and generally make your life extremely difficult.

4. Psychopathic narcissists

I truly hope you never meet one of these characters. They are truly dangerous, showing no empathy or remorse, and actively seek to impose suffering on others. Murderers and dangerous abusers fall into this category. They enjoy the suffering of others and are vampire-like in their consumption of misery and pain.

The 4 Types of People That Narcissists Are Attracted to

One thing that you need to understand about narcissists is that they have very little sense of self. Instead of developing normal, healthy self-esteem, they ended up as adults feeling that they were both special yet very misunderstood — a strange combination, and not a happy one.

What they are drawn to, like vampires, is people with a good sense of self and a certain empathy towards others. A narcissist will want to both benefit from your kindness and also squash your self-esteem so that you give them more of your energy. They feed on the good feelings of others because they have none of their own to draw upon.

One of the terms you will hear in relation to narcissists is "supply." But what is it? Essentially, **narcissistic supply** is what they want from you — supply to them is attention, drama, focus, energy. You may have heard the phrase "she was sucking the life out of me." This is what being around a narcissist for any length of time feels like — you feel compelled to give them so much of yourself, while getting very little back, and you end up feeling exhausted.

Here are 4 of the features found in those who fall prey to the mind games of the narcissist. Keep in mind, though, that you don't have to give in to them. If you learn to spot a narcissist, you can put up good boundaries and protect yourself. In the following chapters, we'll show you how.

1. **Someone successful and talented**

Although you'll never get the narcissist to admit it, they may target you because they perceive you to be successful or talented in some way. Unable to deal with their feelings of jealousy, they will then make a game of bringing you down, humiliating you and destroying your confidence as a way of feeling better about themselves.

Does this actually work for them? No. But remember, the narcissist is very immature. They are like a four-year-old stamping on another child's sandcastle, which they wish they had built themselves. Taking someone else down may give them some temporary relief, but soon enough, those feelings of jealousy and inadequacy will return. If you're around when they do, prepare to be attacked once again. This is the cycle of narcissistic abuse, and you will soon come to recognize that the good days are always followed by bad ones.

Narcissists will also be drawn to successful people because they feel they can ride on your coattails and draw on your connections and talents to benefit themselves — for example, turning up at your professional events and using their connection with you to meet people and try to advance their own interests.

2. **Someone who makes the narcissist feel OK about themselves**

Again, you'll find that people who feel good about themselves tend to be willing to lend that same energy to others. So they'll give people compliments or reach out with kind gestures in the belief that this is just how you behave in life. Unfortunately for them, the narcissist will want more and more of these kindnesses, until the giver feels drained and exhausted by them. Narcissists are bottomless pits of need, and if you give them a hand, they'll take an arm.

Again, I can't emphasize enough how important it is to look not at someone's words — which can be very charming when necessary — but at how you feel around them. Do you feel on edge? Do you feel exhausted? If you are someone who tends to be kind and giving, be aware that sometimes, for your own sake, you need to hold back.

3. Someone who makes them look good

It's not about you; it's about them. So if you have some talent, or are good looking, or impressive in some way, you may find a narcissist attaching themselves to you and feeding off your reflected glory. You may find the attention flattering, but after a while, you'll want to shake them off. That's when you realize it's not as straightforward as dealing with a normal person.

4. Someone who indulges them and puts up with their behavior

Be careful of being too kind or understanding with a narcissist. While normal people won't take advantage of your kindness, you can be sure that this personality type will. They will essentially feed off your goodwill and attention, needing more and more of it. And if you attempt to back off or set some boundaries, be prepared for trouble.

So there you have it. With this chapter, we've looked at what makes someone a narcissist and what kinds of people they are drawn to. Read on to find out what to do if you have just realized you have a narcissist in your life!

Chapter 2 - Staying One Step Ahead

Narcissists are very skilled at manipulation, so it's all too easy to miss the early warning signs that you're in a dangerous situation with someone who seems perfectly normal and charming.

What you can arm yourself with, however, are some signs to look out for when you've just met someone and are wondering if it's "all in your head" or not. Narcissists are not quite as clever as they think they are, and you will soon learn to spot some common traits and signals.

In this chapter, we'll also look at some of the tactics used by narcissists to manipulate you, and some of the common phrases you are likely to hear from this personality type.

Finally, we'll look at narcissistic rage and its triggers. This is an important section to read as, if you haven't experienced it before, a narcissistic rage can come as a huge shock. You'll be left wondering what you've done wrong and how you can fix it.

11 Ways to Know You're in a Relationship with a Narcissist

1. They seem absolutely lovely at the start
You know what they say about something or someone that seems too good to be true. They usually are. If someone is so sweet, agreeable, and utterly delighted by everything you say and do, it should leave you feeling a little... wary. No one is that nice, right? When is this going to turn?

Trust your instincts. This cannot be stressed enough. You may be falling prey to **love bombing**, which is just what it sounds like — being absolutely smothered in love and admiration.

Don't just look at what someone says or does. Look into their eyes — does their expression match their words? Narcissists can be incredibly sweet and charming, but they can't hide their cold eyes. So, if you feel like someone's words and expression aren't quite adding up, believe yourself.

Narcissists don't want the same things from a relationship that ordinary people want. While you or I may look for company, conversation, support and shared laughter, a narcissist is focused only on what they can get from you — be that attention, glory, time, energy, money and status.

They tend to see others only in terms of what they can do for the narcissist, not as someone to share a mutually supportive relationship. So when someone seems determined to win you over, to be bombarding you with texts and declarations of affection, take a step back. Enjoy the attention, certainly, but take it with a grain of salt. Time will tell.

2. They are incredibly selfish
This is a trait shared by all narcissists, and one that plays out in big ways and small. Notice what they're like to be around — are you the one doing all the listening, or do they listen back (and by that I mean, active listening, reflecting what you say and genuinely seeming to engage with you as a person)?

Do you end up giving more — more money, more work, more emotional energy? When you come away from them, do you feel inspired and uplifted, or simply drained. A narcissist may be charming and funny, but they also have a way of taking up all the available oxygen in a room, of making everything about them. You may not notice this right away, particularly if you are someone who likes to give, but just start to notice and you may see a pattern of selfish behavior emerging.

Another point here: look at how they behave when no one is around. They may be good at the grand gestures when they have an audience, but how do they treat you when it's just the two of you?

3. They care more about the image of your relationship than the reality

Again, this is about the narcissist's obsession with appearances. Narcissists tend to be both secretive and obsessed with their public image. You may have been arguing with them that morning, but they will still post a loved-up picture of the two of you to their social media accounts and present a perfect image of your relationship to others.

With most people, life is shades of gray. But with this personality type, their need to be the best, the most popular, successful, and attractive trumps their need for any kind of authenticity. One of the things that come as a surprise to people in a relationship with a narcissist is that when they talk to others about how badly the relationship is going, they are often met with surprise.

"But she always speaks so highly of you!" is a common response. This is because narcissists want to give the impression of getting along with everyone and of sharing a wonderful intimacy with you to others. As well as wanting to preserve their image of themselves as a wonderful, popular person, this also means that others don't believe you when you say that the relationship is not as wonderful as it seems. So you end up feeling both isolated and confused — are you imagining things? (The answer is no.)

4. They are critical of everything you do

A narcissist likes to control others to feel more secure themselves, and one way of doing that is to criticize and find fault with everything that you do. The result is that you feel on edge, like you're walking on eggshells, toning yourself down to avoid further negative comments.

Be wary of those little comments about what you're wearing, your hair, your career choices, and small daily decisions — they may seem harmless on their own, but they can start to add up and chip away at your self-esteem, which makes the narcissist far more powerful than you.

If you're in a romantic partnership, look at how someone was at the start of your relationship — did they find everything you did wonderful? If that starts to change, you can doubt yourself. What are you doing wrong? How can you fix it, to get it back to how it was at the start.

Stop these thoughts! The problem isn't you.

5. You can't argue with them

With normal people, arguing may not be pleasant, but with a bit of give and take, you can either agree to disagree or move on to other topics.

Not so with a narcissist! They are simply unable to compromise or to acknowledge that they are wrong. Getting them to back down is even more challenging, and they never, ever apologize. Why would they? Doing that would be admitting they aren't perfect, and for the narcissist that is impossible to even contemplate.

6. If you disagree, you're the problem

Narcissistic Relationship

Part of the narcissist's inability to ever admit they have crossed a line or done something wrong (which they frequently do) is that if you do disagree with them, you won't just be met with a flat refusal to acknowledge their mistake. Instead, you'll find yourself in the wrong and being attacked. Here's an example:

You: I really felt when we were out tonight that you were quite rude to me in front of my friends, and it made me feel bad.

The Narcissist: I don't know what you're talking about. That's not true. Why are you like this all the time — so angry and oversensitive?

See the difference? A normal person would listen, reflect on their behavior, and apologize. A narcissist will not only reject what you are saying; they will go further and make out that you're the one with emotional problems.

7. They don't have any close friends

A narcissist may have a lot of people around them who admire them, joke with them on social media and like their numerous selfies on Instagram. But do they have old school friends? People who have been in their life for a long time? Or is it all just superficial?

Narcissists tend to burn a lot of bridges, so if you meet someone and they appear to have no old friends at all, take note. It may be that they treat everyone so badly they are unable to maintain long relationships.

8. All their exes are crazy

As a general rule, if you hear this, run a mile. Often, the ex may well have been driven a bit crazy by the narcissist's behavior, but has since recovered and moved on. If someone seems obsessed with talking about their ex and his or her craziness, it's a big red alarm bell, and you should listen. Or you will be the next crazy one.

Also beware of the person who places all the blame on a failed relationship with the ex. Usually, a relationship fails because of shared problems or differences. It's rare for one person to be all bad and the other to be blameless. If this is how an ex is being presented, you may be in the presence of a narcissist.

9. They are suddenly nicer when you pull back
Narcissists are emotional vampires. They don't care about you as a person, but they do care, very much, about having access to your time, money, presence, and energy.

If someone treats you badly or suddenly shows their true self, it's natural to pull away. The other party may notice and apologize, perhaps, and you will both move on. With a narcissist, though, they are incapable of apology and reflection.

What they will do, though, is lure you back with kindness, extra attention, and charm. You'll know deep down that you're being played, but you'll also welcome the more reasonable behavior, feel relieved, and seek to move past it. And so the cycle will begin again.

10. They'll fight hard when you leave them
Relationships end, and it's sometimes a struggle to leave on good terms. But if a relationship has run its course, it can be done, particularly if both parties are committed to being kind and getting on with their own lives. Try and get away from a narcissist, however, and be prepared for a lot of resistance.

You may find yourself bombarded with phone calls, text messages, and even have them turning up at your door. They will also send in "flying monkeys" —people who believe the narcissist's version of events and will be convinced by the narcissist to call you up and elicit feelings of guilt and obligation to give the narcissist yet another chance. Even if they don't particularly want to be with you anymore, they will keep you dangling because they don't want to see you with anyone else.

Sometimes people decide that it's actually easier to just give in for the sake of a peaceful life — particularly if other people are being drawn into the drama — and so the cycle begins again. Once you have let them back, you can be certain that the cycle of indifference and nastiness will start again. Soon, you will probably find yourself being punished at some point for trying to break free at all.

11. You feel bad about yourself when you are around them

It's been said that you may forget what someone said to you, but you'll never forget how they made you feel. If someone makes you feel exhausted, drained, irritable, depressed, or insecure, take note. These are never good signs in a relationship.

A genuine narcissist can also make you feel frightened — in their body language and in the energy they are giving off. While their words may be conveying one thing, their physical presence and their eyes may be saying something quite different.

It's always worth listening to your gut in these situations and taking note of your bodily reactions as well as your more logical thoughts — they are equally important, and often your gut instinct is spot on.

If you notice yourself feeling anxious or on edge around someone, they may not be a narcissist, but you still need to acknowledge those feelings and set appropriate boundaries, even disengage gracefully. You don't need to have a huge showdown — sometimes, simply turning down the volume on a relationship is all you need to do to protect yourself.

Dangerous Manipulation Tactics Used by Narcissists

Narcissists have a number of tactics they use regularly to lure you into their world and keep you there. What is different from ordinary relationships is that there is always an element of control with a narcissist.

While in a typical relationship there is give and take, and a gradual building of intimacy and trust, with a narcissist it all unfolds in a way that leaves you emotionally vulnerable, weakened and at a real disadvantage. Look out for these tactics in your relationship and see if you notice anything familiar — if you do, you may well need to get yourself out of your current situation.

1.   Intermittent reinforcement

This is when someone treats you nicely, but only *sometimes*. You may put up with all kinds of shabby behavior — turning up late, showing little interest in your life, catty remarks and bullying — and then every so often, you are floored by how kind, loving, and understanding they can be.

This has a noticeable effect on your mental state. You'll feel quietly undermined by them, by their comments and behavior. You'll start to question your every move and walk on eggshells around them to avoid further criticism. You may even find yourself constantly thinking of ways to please them.

After a while, though, you might suddenly feel like you've had enough. Nothing you do seems to please them. You spend time with other people and realize how odd their behavior is in comparison. You start to wonder if perhaps you'd be better off creating some distance.

Bingo! At this point, **intermittent reinforcement** will kick in. You'll be suddenly floored by how understanding, receptive, and incredibly nice they are being. Just when you start to relax and think, *wow, they are really lovely*, the bad behavior will start again. This is a very clever tool, because people are naturally wired to go back for more when someone leaves them hanging.

Treat them mean, keep them keen, does, unfortunately, work for many of us. Another word for this tactic is **hoovering** — once they know they've gone too far, they'll start trying to hoover you back under their thumb with unexpected kindness and sweet-talking.

But this is no way to live and takes a huge emotional toll. If someone is nice to you, but only *sometimes*, take note. It's not healthy or normal behavior, and you deserve so much more. In genuine relationships, people treat each other well. If they don't, for some reason, they acknowledge it and apologize. If you find yourself being treated badly by those close to you, there's a big problem.

2. **Gaslighting**

This term *gaslighting* derives from the 1944 movie, *Gaslight*. In it, the abusive husband cleverly manipulates his wife into believing she is going crazy by changing her environment in all sorts of subtle ways. In her house, gaslights dim for no apparent reason, things go missing, pictures vanish from walls. She never quite knows if things are changing around her or if it's all in her head. Narcissists **gaslight** those around them regularly in all sorts of ways.

Gaslighters cause you to doubt your own sanity and keep you on unsteady ground by telling blatant lies that they then deny, making out that you are the crazy one. Some examples of gaslighting in a modern relationship might be:

Example one:

Your gaslighter tells you some unpleasant fact about yourself — for example, that you once slapped him across the face — and when you say, *no I never did that*, they say — *but you did!*

You wonder if you have simply forgotten it, or if you really did slap him across the face. You know that it's not in your nature to hit someone — yet he seems so confident that it's true. Who is right?

Example two:

Your gaslighter says he will take you out for lunch on the weekend. When you bring it up to arrange a time, he says, *no, I never agreed to that. I'm busy all weekend.*

You don't want to push it, because you know how upset he can get if he's challenged, but at the same time, you were looking forward to it. And surely, if he offered it, he would remember. Ultimately, it's easier just to let it go, but it leaves you feeling oddly mistreated.

Example three:

Gaslighting can also take place around boundaries. Let's say your friend asks if they can stay with you for a week. When after two weeks they show no signs of leaving and you push them for a definite end date, they fly into a rage about how unreasonable and unwelcoming you are being.

You wonder if you are being unreasonable. After all, they said they were only coming for a week, and now it's been two. Surely that's reasonable to ask? But they seem so angry, so maybe it is rude of you?

Maybe you are being selfish, as they say. No it's not, and no you're not. You are being gaslit.

It's important to note here that people can forget what they said or be vague for other perfectly harmless reasons. But watch out if you start to notice a pattern — what is being said seems to change constantly, or you don't remember saying or doing certain things that you are being accused of, or feel like you are being manipulated somehow.

Gaslighting is incredibly difficult to call out because it's the work of people who are setting out to deceive you deliberately, not the work of fair and reasonable human beings. Really, the best thing to do if you notice gaslighting is to leave — you will never win with someone who refuses to play fair.

3.   Projection

Anything a narcissist doesn't like about themselves, they will project onto you and others. So while narcissists are some of the most selfish people you will ever meet, they are also the first to accuse others of being selfish. This may be people in their circle, or it may be politicians or public figures.

For example, a female narcissist may make frequent comments about "all men being a bit stupid," but is the first to cry sexism if a man doesn't shower them with admiration and undivided attention.

They will also accuse you of being a liar if you call them out on their own lies. You will never, ever hear an admission of guilt. All you will hear is a flat denial, followed up by a declaration that you are unfairly targetting them with *your* lies.

Narcissists are unable to reflect on their behavior and admit that they are in the wrong. Far easier to dump the blame and attending shame on you, and view themselves as the wounded party.

4. Nonsensical conversations

With most people, if you have an issue you'd like to discuss with them — perhaps to do with their treatment of you or your relationship — you would expect them to listen, reflect, and respond appropriately. Not so the narcissist! (Do you see a pattern yet?)

One of their most infuriating tactics is to shower you with **word salad** when you try and have a conversation with them about some aspect of their behavior that you are finding difficult. Prepare to be bombarded with bizarre observations, unrelated anecdotes, and strangely worded sentences that don't make much sense. You'll leave the conversation thinking — "What just happened?" while the narcissist goes on their merry way, knowing full well what they have done.

If you confront them, you'll be met with a flat denial. And, most likely, another generous serve of word salad. So really, there's no point getting into any kind of disagreement with a narcissist. It's like trying to argue with a toddler — you get nowhere.

Another thing to note here is that narcissists enjoy confrontation and argument. It fires them up to win and to leave you feeling like the bad guy. So the best thing to do is to avoid arguing with them at all — and further along, we'll learn some tactics for doing just this.

5. Vague or overt threats

Narcissists tend to be possessive and jealous, but they won't always come out and admit they are feeling this way. Instead, you'll receive a vague sense of unease if you do something they don't approve of — sulking, an angry tone, or a tantrum accompanied by threats.

Things that you would expect your friends to celebrate — a new job, some exciting personal news — will leave them feeling inadequate and abandoned. They don't like the success of others, as it draws attention away from them, so they will find all kinds of ways to burst your balloon.

If you feel you have to walk on eggshells around someone for fear of their anger, or if you stop doing things you'd ordinarily enjoy, such as going out with your friends because you're worried that you'll get in trouble, take note. This is not normal or fair behavior, and it reflects the narcissist's childish desire to have you always focused on them, and not on other things or people that make you happy.

Yes, it's a shame they react so badly, particularly if the narcissist is a family member, for example. But they won't change, so the best thing to do is to only share your good news with those you know will want to celebrate along with you. Ignore any threats and call out any sulking — you don't need to put up with it.

6. Baiting, shaming, insulting and name-calling

All of these tactics are used by narcissists, often in subtle ways that leave you wondering if you are oversensitive or just imagining things. Narcissists love to **bait**, which means saying something with the intention of hitting your weak spots or provoking anger. You take the bait, and suddenly you're being difficult and creating a drama out of nothing.

While most people, even if they know your weak spots (and we all have them) will take care to tread carefully around them, narcissists are the opposite. They will learn the things you feel sensitive about and take great pleasure in making you feel worse about them, all to make themselves feel more powerful.

Insulting and **shaming** are the same kinds of tactics — a narcissist will skilfully uncover your weak spots or things you feel self-conscious about, and then use this knowledge to insult and shame you later on. Often, this may be in the form of jokes, so that if you dare complain, you will be told you don't have a sense of humor, adding insult to injury.

5 Things Every Narcissist Likes to Say

Narcissists have a very predictable playbook, and because their tactics are so similiar, you will often here the same statements from them again and again.

1.   **"That didn't happen." and "You're imagining it."**
These are both classic narcissists statements that underpin much of their gaslighting, as I described above. If you question something the narcissist has said or done in the past, perhaps in light of new information and because it contradicts what they are saying now, they will simply deny it. Denial is one of their first defenses because unlike normal people, they have no qualms about outright lying to save their own skin.

If you can prove without a doubt that they did do something, their final defense will be that you deserved it, often for spurious or unrelated reasons (remember that they also use **word salad**).

2.   **"You're crazy."**
Because narcissists are unable to accept their ordinary flaws and vulnerabilities, be prepared to be told you're crazy if you dare question their version of events. They may not come right out and say this, but

you might find yourself being reminded of that time you got very down, or they might refer in general terms to people who are crazy but in a way that makes you suspect they are referring to you in particular.

3. "You're oversensitive."

If a narcissist goes too far in what they say or how they treat you, don't ever expect them to apologize. They are, in their own eyes, incapable of being wrong, so an apology is beneath them.

What you will hear, however, is that you are overly sensitive. Or unreasonable. Or that you have always been a bit fragile. Or again, they will mention some other time when you showed emotional vulnerability, as a way of reminding you that you aren't as strong or capable as they are (although, of course, showing vulnerability isn't weak, it's normal human behavior).

4. "It was just a joke! I'm *joking*."

As well as being oversensitive, if you take offense at one of the narcissist's cruel barbs, be prepared to find out that you have "no sense of humor" or that you "can't take a joke."

Of course, you could retaliate by pointing out that what they said wasn't actually funny, it was just nasty, bullying or plain rude, but if you do, prepare for more defensive behavior.

5. "In my experience..."

Or variations of the above, but essentially, if you talk about something that's happening in your life, perhaps a career success or anecdote, the narcissist will always be able to top it.

If you wrote a book, they wrote a bestseller. If you had a baby, they had five. This applies not just to achievements, but also drama. If you had your purse stolen, they stood up to a bank robber and saved someone's life. What is happening here is that the narcissist is unable to bear the attention being diverted from them — they want to be centered at all times, they want to be better, they want to be the hero in every story.

You may not realize this at first, so you talk a little about yourself as well as asking the right questions and listening. But you'll soon learn to keep quiet about your own achievements because if you speak up, you'll be put in your place with a ten-minute monologue about how they did it better. It becomes easier just to keep quiet and spare yourself the boredom of listening to their boasting (again.)

5 Triggers for Narcissistic Rage

So what is narcissistic rage? Think of it as the grown-up, much scarier version of a toddler temper tantrum. While most of us get angry from time to time, we are usually able to soothe ourselves, calm down, and take steps to handle our anger without lashing out at others or doing permanent damage to our relationships.

A narcissist's rage, however, is something else entirely. These personalities just loathe being told off or challenged. Being confronted or triggered about their shortcomings is not pleasant for anyone, but it's unbearable to them, and you will be met with such seething fury that you may feel physically assaulted. Ideally, according to the narcissist, you will learn your lesson and not do it again.

Or you will be met with icy silence and quiet passive-aggressive fuming. What you won't get is a clear explanation of what's going on or a way forward.

Narcissistic Relationship

So what incites narcissistic rage? Essentially, anything that threatens their view of themselves as a perfect, successful, and extraordinarily special human being.

Here are some surefire ways to find out just how angry a narcissist can get:

1. You confront them on their behavior

If you call a narcissist out on their behavior, prepare to suffer. Even if you make your feelings known in a way that's constructive and diplomatic, you have broken the unspoken rule that the narcissist is never wrong.

Be prepared for flat out denial, rage, projection, and blame, but be assured that you will never see any form of acknowledgment that you have a point, and perhaps they could do things differently next time. If you really do have a point and they have no reasonable defense for their behavior, their final tactic is to collapse in a heap and cry, so you look (and feel) like the bad guy.

2. You ignore them

If you realize you are in a relationship with a narcissist and decide, for your own mental health, to back away or take some space from them, prepare to be challenged. Above all else, narcissists hate to be ignored, and if you set some reasonable boundaries around their access to you, expect them to be trampled on.

Often, this may be with someone, perhaps a family member or lackluster romantic partner, who typically shows little interest in your life, makes no effort to be around you, and makes unpleasant comments or criticism of your life choices.

But should you back off or start avoiding them, that will change. Expect to be bombarded with phone calls, emails and even unannounced visits to your home. This is because you are never allowed to call the shots with a narcissist, and you must always make them the center of attention.

And while they don't enjoy being around people in the normal sense, they also need you to give them **narcissistic supply**, which, as we have covered, is essentially your attention and energy. Should you try and take that away from them, they respond like addicts being deprived of what they need. Eventually, they will give up and move on to someone else. But before that happens, prepare yourself for a fight!

3.   You laugh at them

One thing that narcissists value above all else is their public image as someone who is special, intelligent, and high status. While most people are capable of being self-deprecating or laughing at themselves from time to time, this is impossible for a narcissist. This is because it touches on their deep shame and hidden insecurity as someone who is ordinary, sometimes frightened, and not particularly special or talented. Laugh at them and prepare to be met with cold fury.

4.   They don't get special treatment

Narcissists often have the people around them very well trained to treat them as if they are special and unique. But often, when they confront strangers, it doesn't go quite as they would like. They may demand special treatment from shop staff, or sit in first class when they have a third-class ticket.

When this happens, the unsuspecting stranger will soon find out just how 'special' the narcissist is and find themselves on the receiving end of verbal abuse or just more demands for attention that the narcissist actually needs or wants — they just want to make that person pay attention to them. They are the kinds of people to make rambling complaints to customer services departments, to badmouth companies with unfair reviews and to complain at length about poor customer service rather than shrugging their shoulders and taking their business elsewhere.

In personal relationships, you can also expect to see narcissistic rage if you pull back or refuse to pay special attention to the narcissist.

5.   You take center stage

Let's say it's your birthday, and you want to celebrate with a meal or a birthday cake. While most people are happy to let the birthday girl or boy be the center of attention for one day, narcissists find this unbearable. Prepare for extra demands, sulking, an inexplicable tantrum or catty comments — because of course, it's all about them.

Another strange and noticeable feature of narcissists is that they are generally very bad gift-givers. Going out, choosing something that someone would love, wrapping it and presenting it to them is not something that narcissists see as worth doing. Of course, this alone doesn't mean that someone is a narcissist, but it's a common enough trait that it's worth mentioning.

What is the impact of the narcissist on you?

This is an interesting question, and one worth asking yourself. Surely, people can be difficult. Is it worth disrupting a marriage or romantic relationship or cutting regular contact with a parent because they are a narcissist? Is it not better, for the sake of peace, to simply put up with them? Breaking up families, leaving parents behind, leaving your boyfriend or girlfriend — these are all big decisions to make with life-changing consequences.

Narcissistic Relationship

Is it better to just put up and shut up?

The answer is no. The narcissist will always have you believe that you should put up with them, that they didn't really mean it, that things will be different in the future. But they won't.

And every time you put up with it, every time you bite your tongue and attempt to get over feelings of hurt and disappointment for the sake of an easier life, you are doing two things:

You are affecting your future: your future happiness, your future goals, and aspirations, your children, and grandchildren. Every time you allow the narcissist to beat you down with nasty words and abuse, you are letting him or her rob you of a happier, more peaceful and productive life.

You are also affecting your own health and wellbeing in the moment. Of course, you just want the behavior to stop, for things to go back to normal. The easiest way to achieve that is to let the narcissist win. But play the long game. You can't see the impact of long-term, low-level stress and abuse on your mental health, but be certain it is having an impact. You have a choice to change things. And you deserve so much better.

Read on to find out how you can choose better for yourself.

Narcissistic Relationship

Chapter 3 - When Enough Is Enough

So if you've read this far, you may have realized you have a narcissist in your life. The question for you now is, what are you going to do about it?

It may not be practical to break ties with them completely — perhaps you work with them, or they are a family member and the fall out will be too great if you cut them off completely — but what you need to do now is put your foot down. You need to change how you deal with them and prepare yourself for pushback. You need some strategies under your belt, and you need to believe in yourself enough to carry them out. Most of all, you need to heal, to practice self-care and to ensure that you set good boundaries so that you are safe from harm in the future.

You'll also learn about the Connection Contract and how this can help you get your own needs met. You may find, ultimately, that this is the first step in freeing yourself completely from a narcissist.

Read on to find out how to deal with a narcissist and protect yourself while they are still in your life.

5 Essential Tips for Dealing with a Narcissist the Right Way

Before we go much further, it's worth learning the five essential tips that you can keep in mind when dealing with narcissists. Remember, you are dealing with someone who does not have an ordinary personality. They don't follow the normal rules for human interaction, so you need to treat them differently, too. Most importantly, you need to protect yourself from harm as you set about breaking away. Here's how:

1. Keep quiet and carry on

If you are working with a narcissist, for example, you may feel like you're the only one who noticed just how superficial their charm really is. It may even be tempting to confront them, or out them to others.

Don't. Bide your time, keep your guard up around them, don't share any secrets and remain pleasant and just a little distant. In time, the narcissist's mask with start to slip and they will reveal their true selves to others. At this point, you can watch from a safe distance. But you can't force this process without putting yourself in harm's way.

If you try and make this happen faster, you run the risk of inciting their narcissistic rage and having them turn on you, and you want to avoid that at all costs for your own wellbeing.

Remember, narcissists don't play fair, and they hate being confronted with their own shortcomings. It's a game you won't win unless you stoop to their level — and who wants to do that — so simply refuse to play. You'll be on your way to making your escape, and the longer the narcissist remains unaware of your plans, the smoother your exit will be. Keep quiet, build your escape plan, and work on your own wellbeing — which we will cover in future chapters.

2. Disengage

Ultimately, what a narcissist wants is attention. Like a toddler, if they aren't getting positive attention, they will soon move onto behaving badly. If you consistently refuse to get drawn into their games, though, they will simply move on to someone else who is more willing to take the bait.

If you spot a narcissist, take things slowly and if you are proved right, be as boring as you can when talking to them. This is a great way to both protect yourself and hopefully see the back of them, too.

In some situations, you may not want to be boring. For example, in your professional life, you may want to shine and if your narcissist is in the same field, you may have to deal with some jealousy. Simply focus on doing your own work as best you can, never bite back, and be polite and professional at all times.

In personal relationships, start to step back a little, gradually. Stop taking the bait in arguments, stop expecting them to change, keep conversations light.

3. Work our your boundaries and make them clear

This is something you may need to do if you have realized you are in a relationship with a narcissist. These personalities constantly push boundaries in all kinds of ways — imposing on your time, your energy, your privacy and your personal life. Once you recognize this, however, you'll be in a stronger position to set and maintain boundaries around what is important to you.

For example, let's say a relative constantly makes negative or belittling comments about your career. Knowing this, have a few set phrases ready when the next comment comes: such as, "Hmm. I am really happy with how my work is going. It's not always a smooth road, but I feel like I'm making progress." Deliver them lightly, without any heat at all, and know that you have just made a choice to stand up for yourself that strengthens your position and weakens that of the narcissist.

And then change the subject, or put it back onto them and ask them about how their work is going.

Or perhaps the narcissist tries to draw you into a conversation about how your life is going, and you sense some probing. Be aware that narcissists like to learn your weak spots so they can reveal them to others or bait you with them at some later date.

In this case, again, remain friendly and neutral while giving nothing away that you don't want to — remember, just because someone has asked you a personal question it doesn't mean you have to answer it. Sometimes, simply replying with "What do you mean?" or "Why do you ask?" will put an end to their fishing.

4.   Don't expect fair or reasonable behavior

Narcissists are chronic game players. But they also tend to have predictable methods of attack and will try the same thing again and again if they see it gets a rise out of you. Be unpredictable in response, and work on your own strategies, which might be as simple as refusal.

If they make a nasty comment, simply refuse to accept it. State mildly, "No. That's not true."

Never expect them to be fair or kind, and have your guard up ready to bounce back. Even a long pause followed by "What do you mean?" is effective and gives you time in the moment to stand up for yourself.

Leave them feeling slightly unsure about whether you're wise to them or not. They will never play fair, so don't feel like you have to be completely fair in response — play them at their own game, but innocently.

Another good tactic here, if you have to work with a narcissist, perhaps, or see one at a family gathering, is to prepare yourself in advance. Get a good night's sleep, eat well, get some exercise and learn some simple breathing techniques that will help you remain calm and cheerful in the moment. Narcissists tend to prey on the weak, so keeping yourself strong and healthy is a good way of fending them off. We'll look more at this later on.

5. Accept them

This is a hard thing to do, particularly if you are very attached to your narcissist — if, perhaps, they are your romantic partner, close friend, or parent. But if you can accept that they are a narcissist, that they cannot change and that you will never get anything different from them, your life will be easier. Part of the frustration of this personality type is that they can be so nice at times. You know they have it in them, so why can't they be like that all the time?

It doesn't matter. They can't. Often, they have no incentive to change. After all, the life of a narcissist is often superficially quite pleasant, especially with a few trained monkeys dancing around him or her. Yes, they have their demons, but they keep them well buried so mostly they are fairly content.

Accepting that your narcissist will not change is the first step in moving forward with your own life, free of their negative influence. You may not be able to shake them off entirely if they are a family member, but you will find they spend much less time under your skin than they are used to.

If you are in a romantic relationship with a narcissist, giving up on your expectations that they will change is the first step to freeing yourself, and moving on without them, or accepting them for who they are and finding other ways to get your needs met. You deserve better, after all.

5 Phrases to Instantly Disarm a Narcissist

1.   "I agree." or "You're so right."

If you are in a work situation or family celebration, it's far easier to just go along with the narcissist. Agree with whatever they say, smile sweetly and be ever so slightly boring so that they quickly move on to someone else for more drama.

Challenging a narcissist is never really worth the energy as you will end up feeling attacked and unworthy if you do so — they cannot tolerate it, and if you try, you will soon realize just how difficult it is for them. What's more, they will seek to win the argument at any cost, and you will end up feeling attacked. Far better to smile sweetly and move on to other things — such as doing something that will make you feel good.

2.   "What will people think?"

One thing the narcissist values about all else is their image. If you want them to do something for you or just behave themselves, be sure to remind them that their behavior will be visible to others.

One of way doing this is inviting other people into a situation. Let's say you're arguing with them. Say, "Look, I think I'll have a chat to so-and-so about this and see what they think" or, "Should we get Dad into the room too so we can talk about this together." They will quickly change their tune if they realize you are prepared to make others aware of their behavior and not keep it quiet.

3. "I'm sorry you feel that way."

This is a great way to defuse an argument with a narcissist. It puts their feelings firmly back onto them and is neutral enough to discourage further attacks. You aren't apologizing or taking the blame, but you are acknowledging that it is hard for them to be challenged.

4. "I can live with your faulty perception of me"

Again, this is putting the narcissist's feelings and opinions back onto them. Let's say you have set a clear boundary with a narcissist that they aren't happy with. Now, they are attacking you and saying that you're being difficult and awkward and that you should give in to them.

Instead of saying, "No I'm not!" and getting into a defensive mode, stating calmly that you can accept their faulty opinion does two things: It tells them that they are wrong, but you aren't going to bother trying to correct them. Instead, you are going to accept that *they* are wrong, and move on. It leaves them with nowhere to go because you aren't taking on their negative attitude towards you.

Essentially, you are saying that you have no interest in controlling their thoughts, even though you don't agree with them or accept them in any way — which is a healthy attitude to take towards anyone, really.

5. "Your anger is not my responsibility."

Again, you are putting their behavior back on to them. This one may make them absolutely furious — narcissists tend to hate any form of self-help talk or what they see as new-age nonsense. Just repeat this back to them, more than once if necessary, and get away from them if you can. They will soon get bored and move on.

How to Protect Yourself from a Narcissist

Protecting yourself from a narcissist isn't easy, but there are a few tactics you can try. If you aren't yet ready to leave a relationship with a narcissist, you may want to consider forming a **connection contract** with them to get what you want from the relationship.

What's a connection contract?

Put simply, a connection contract is a written agreement setting out your baseline for how you wish to be treated. Should the narcissist break this contract, they no longer have the right to enjoy a connection with you. If you are in a relationship with a narcissist, it may read something like this:

"I don't want to listen to putdowns or be yelled at or criticized unfairly. If you are incapable of doing this, I will leave."

For a narcissistic parent who wishes to visit you, it might be more like this:

"You can stay at my house for three nights, but while you are here you are to engage positively with my children, and not yell or scream to me or anyone else who lives here. Nor do I want to give you money — you need to handle your own finances and pay for your own expenses at all times. If you can't agree to these conditions, you will need to pay for a hotel and we can meet for coffee."

Essentially, a connection contract creates a crystal-clear and neutral set of guidelines about what will be tolerated and what won't. If the narcissist breaches this, you don't need to get angry or argue, you simply point out that they have broken the contract and therefore they are no longer welcome in your presence.

Yes, it's tough and it's blunt, but it takes the pressure off you to constantly be wondering what is acceptable and what isn't. With a connection contract, everyone knows what the rules are, and if the narcissist breaks them (and chances are, they will), you can point to the contract and keep your cool.

When is it appropriate to use a connection contract?

A connection contract may come in handy when you have already had several blowups and confrontations with a narcissist, and they know that you are not happy with their behavior but they are unwilling to change or acknowledge that they have done anything wrong.

Essentially, it takes over from the arguing and sets out what you don't see as acceptable. They might read it and want to argue again, in which case you can simply say that you don't want to argue further, you just want to go with what's written down.

It's a final way of trying to get a narcissist to behave themselves, and while it may not be successful, it does at least show that you mean business.

Chapter 4 - Cutting the Cord

Why It's So Hard to Break up with a Narcissist

Let's say you've read this far and realized you are in a relationship that is toxic to your own wellbeing, and you need to get out. This may be someone you have been in a romantic relationship with, or it may be a family member or close friend you need to back away from. Whatever the situation, you need to follow some trusted strategies to protect yourself while you go through with this process.

One thing you need to bear in mind as you make plans is that getting out of a relationship with a narcissist is **not like breaking up with most people**. They don't like it, and they will make it extremely hard for you.

If you have fallen for a narcissist, you will be enmeshed in what psychologists refer to as a trauma bond. As humans, we are wired to feel close to others. So the narcissist's tactic of love bombing at the start of a relationship, or when we start to pull back, will naturally make you feel closer to them.

But eventually, a narcissist will slowly but surely turn on you. You will feel confused and insecure because you never quite know where you stand. This uncertainty makes you less confident and easier to manipulate — all tactics that the narcissist will employ without conscience to gain the upper hand in the relationship. You will feel confused because you had bonded to them in one of their nicer moments and now you are seeing a different side to them.

Narcissistic Relationship

You may know the relationship is bad for you and that this person makes you unhappy or fearful, but somehow you have lost the courage to look after yourself and leave. You're also doubting yourself — after all, you seemed to make them so happy at first? Surely for things to change, you must have done something wrong, and if you could just work out what it was, you will get things back to how they were? And every so often they are utterly lovely, which keeps you hanging on.

Narcissists are also very good at isolating their victims, so you may feel like you have no one to turn to. This isn't true. Chances are, there are old friends or family who will embrace you if you tell them the truth about your relationship with this person. They may already be aware of the problems and are waiting for you to speak up. The fact is, relationships shouldn't be this hard.

So how did you get into this state? Well, you're human. It happens. Some of us are more vulnerable than others to the charms of the narcissist, and that is something you may need to think about in future — we will look at red flags for future relationships at the end of the book. But essentially, narcissists are very good at what they do, and at creating a trauma bond.

Trauma bonding works a little differently depending on whether it's a long-term relationship — such as with a parent — or a new, romantic partner.

With long-term relationships, it's more of a constant cycle between loving behavior and abuse that can go on for years and is established in childhood.

With romantic relationships, it tends to be that things start off well and deteriorate. Either you get out at the first sign of trouble, or you get caught into an abusive cycle that can go on for years — if you let it.

The 7 Stages of Trauma Bonding

1. Love bombing

You are perfect and you can do no wrong, and you are won over by their charm and attention. They are flattering, kind, affectionate and seem completely in love with you. Of course, being human, you enjoy this. But of course, with the narcissist, it will never last.

2. Trust

You believe everything they are saying, and start to trust and believe in them. While there may be some small part of you that knows it is all a bit too good to be true, they also draw you in with small acts of kindness and intimacy that make you believe and trust them. You've simply never met someone this wonderful before, and they seem to feel the same way!

3. Criticism begins

The love bombing tails off, slowly or sometimes very abruptly, and the nitpicking and criticism start to escalate. Suddenly you are not quite so perfect. This stage may be accompanied by increasing demands on your time and energy, conflict and a feeling of despair or confusion, as you wonder what has changed, and how you can get back on firmer ground again.

4. Gaslighting

This new state of affairs is your fault. If you just did things differently, or you weren't so crazy or irrational, it would all be just fine. You start to doubt yourself, partly because they seem so convincing. They have done nothing wrong. It's all in your head.

5. Control

You go along with what they want because you start to believe that you are in the wrong and this is the only way to get back in their good books.

6. Resignation and increased despair:

Things seem to be getting worse. If you try and fight back, you are met with more abuse. You feel lonely, sad and isolated.

7. You're addicted

You know this person is bad for you, but somehow you keep going back for more, and all you want is to win back their approval and see their kind side. With a parent, this is because we are naturally wired to love our parents, no matter how inadequate they are for the job.

With romantic relationships, it's often because we have a vision for the relationship and its future in our head, and we know it's going to be painful and lonely to give it up and go back to searching again. Far easier to stick it out and hope for things to change. You're also weakened by their constant low-level abuse and not feeling strong enough to get out.

How to Break Up With a Narcissist for Good

Breaking up with a narcissist is not an easy process, but it is worth it. Mainly because the relationship is never going to give you what you need, despite the occasional good day. You are looking for something that just isn't there. Leaving this person behind will free up space and energy in your life for better things, healthier relationships and increased happiness. You are allowed to do that — in fact, I am giving you permission right now! But how do you do it? Read on to find out.

1. Prepare yourself

Get as much information about narcissists as you can. Study this book and other resources, and know that you are doing the right thing for your own wellbeing.

2.   Distance yourself gradually

Be a little less available and a little more boring. Let them think that they are getting bored of you, even, and see if you can slowly disengage rather than letting them realize what you're doing — which can incite narcissistic rage.

3.   Reconnect with others.

This is a great way of breaking the narcissist's hold on you. Find ways of letting others back into your life, no matter how low and isolated you might be feeling. Call up an old friend, go to something that interests you, join a club. Whatever it is, break out of your isolation and surround yourself with healthy people and you'll start to feel better.

4.   Think of an excuse

Try not to make the breakup or distancing about them. Talk about what's better for both of you, and find ways of making it seem more like their idea than yours. Don't fire them up, accuse or tell them their faults — this is unbearable to them and will only make leaving harder.

5.   Make a clean break

Don't drag it out — once you've decided to leave, go quickly. Once you've left, don't contact them again. Stay strong and don't be tempted back by love bombing, which will come. Often, with a family member, it's impossible to make a clean break without a huge amount of disruption within the wider circle of family members. In this case, it's often easier to simply move away or go low contact, which is when you keep contact to a minimum and protect yourself with firm boundaries.

Many children of narcissists will state that the best thing they did was put physical distance between them and their narcissistic parent. It broke the strong emotional hold and also allowed them to really feel safe and happy in a place with no reminders of childhood pain.

6. **Expect and plan for some retaliation**

You'll get people calling you, worried about you — those **flying monkeys** that the narcissist is so good at calling in. You'll get someone else trying to build a bridge. You'll receive phone calls, unexpected visits, letters with insincere apologies in your mailbox. Prepare for all of this and remain strong.

Eventually, if you remain neutral and firm for long enough, the narcissist will get bored and move on to someone else. But it will take time. While that's all going on, put in place some habits to protect you — get lots of sleep, exercise and good food to help you remain calm and focused in the face of the narcissist's outrage. We will cover this later on.

7. **Be kind to yourself**

A relationship with a narcissist can leave you feeling quite drained. You can expect some feelings of grief and a sense of loss, and even failure. These are all normal feelings and they will pass. Give yourself time and space, get some counseling if you need it, and take it easy.

Keeping a journal where you go to unload your feelings and also remind yourself of why you are doing what you are will keep you focused. When the narcissist starts love bombing, read back on your journal to remind yourself of just how nasty they are capable of being, no matter how delightful they are being right now. They won't and can't change, so getting away is the right thing to do. Remind yourself of this when you start to wobble.

Using the Gray Rock Method to Your Advantage

Above all else, narcissists love drama. They are also very competitive and envious, so if you have anything exciting going on in your life they will seek to feed off it — and try and steal away your joy in it. Narcissists love to blow out the candles on someone else's cake.

So how do you deal with this? Don't put the cake in front of them. The Gray Rock Method is a wonderful tool for dealing with narcissists. It goes against our normal instincts, but that's what you need to do when dealing with this personality type.

So how does it work?

Picture a gray rock. No color, no life, nothing to see here. And then, quite simply, behave like one. It's as simple as that. This trick is essentially making yourself appear so dull, so boring, that the narcissist has nothing to feed on and will soon (hopefully) move on to someone else.

What narcissists want is your energy. If you are feeling good, they want to take that from you. If you have some exciting news, they want to top it. If you have something painful going on in your life, they want to get up close and see your pain. They are the true definition of emotional vampires.

Give them nothing but a boring gray rock.

When they come back to you, looking for shiny treasures to steal, continue to give them nothing. Respond to their requests for information with boring small talk. Never tell them what's going well in your life, because they'll find a way to ruin it for you. If they probe, just tell them it's all been pretty quiet. No news.

Gray Rock is a good way of getting yourself written out of the ongoing melodrama that is the narcissist's life. They'll need to go looking elsewhere for their fix, and you'll be free to enjoy a more peaceful existence.

This is hard to do. There's always going to be a part of you that wants to win them over — particularly if they are a parent. After all, aren't they supposed to be happy for their children? Isn't that normal?

Yes, it is normal. The thing you have to remember, though, is that you don't have to be a good person to become a parent. In fact, you can be a thoroughly unpleasant person and have lots of children. It's a sad fact of life that the most undeserving people can be blessed with children, but they are emotionally unequipped to love and care for them.

Thankfully, this isn't the case for most of us. But if you drew the short straw, you are better off accepting it and looking for love and approval elsewhere than trying to get it from someone who doesn't have it in them, even if they are your mother or father.

With a romantic partner, you may find yourself wanting to impress them, to win them over and get things back to how they were at the start. Sadly, you can't. Their initial charm was an act, and what you are seeing now is their true self. Stop trying to win them over, and put your energy and time into building a happier future, far away from this damaged soul.

A note for your future self.
Chances are, you won't get into another relationship with a narcissist in a hurry. You have learned your lesson, and you'll know to pull away the minute you see signs of love bombing or sudden nastiness (more on this later.)

But here's a powerful quote from writer Maya Angelou to keep you safe:

"When someone shows you who they are, believe them the first time."

Chapter 5 - Healing From Narcissistic Abuse

If you are reading this book, chances are you are feeling bruised and attacked as a result of the interactions you've had with the narcissist in your life.

Psychologists now recognize that emotional abuse — the kind that you cannot see and leaves its bruises on the soul, not the body — is just as damage and traumatizing as physical abuse. Those who have experienced it often say they would rather be hit physically because wounds to the psyche are far more painful and debilitating.

It's also now recognized that psychological abuse can lead to the same kinds of trauma that result from single traumatic events, such as a burglary or mugging. Because the narcissist's abuse takes place over a long period of time, it can be hard to see the wounds and damage you have sustained. Instead, victims have a feeling of having been attacked or wounded that will take an equally long time to heal from.

Survivors of single incidents like car accidents know this instinctively, and while the damage can be deep, you can recover. The difference with narcissistic abuse, however, is that you may on some level feel it was your fault. The narcissist is very good at making you doubt yourself, at planting little seeds of uncertainty, all the while painting themselves as blameless. It's no wonder you feel like you're under siege or suffering from deep trauma when you encounter a narcissist.

In this, the most important chapter of the book, we will turn our attention from the narcissist and back to where it should be — on you.

We will look at the stages of recovery from narcissistic abuse, and how each one will play out.

We will also reveal the transformative truths that every victim must face up to if they are to recover from their experience. Plus, we will provide you will some essential exercises to strengthen and heal your mind and heart.

Finally, we will offer you life-altering affirmations to heal past hurts and to repeat to yourself like a mantra as you begin the exciting process of moving on from this toxic relationship and starting the next, happier chapter of your life.

The 5 Stages of Recovery from Narcissistic Abuse

Recovering from narcissistic abuse is similar to recovering from the death of a loved one. Particularly if you have loved and believed in this person for a long time and been taken in with their stories, it is hard to accept that they aren't who they said they are in. In fact, they aren't even close to how they portray themselves.

Recovery can be broken down into five stages. To some extent, your healing process will depend on your personality and the narcissist in your life. It's also important to note that there may not be a moment when you say you are completely over what has happened. Abuse leaves scars, and even if they heal over and no new ones are formed, they are still there. But they will make you stronger and more compassionate, so don't feel like you are changed for the worse, or irreversibly damaged. You have simply changed and grown up a little more, as we all do (apart from narcissists!)

Here is a rough guide that will help you understand the recovery process better.

Narcissistic Relationship

Stage 1: Emergency mode

Let's say you've had what you expect to be your final showdown with the narcissist. You've told them it's over, you've left the building or put down the phone, and you are determined that you won't let them back again.

You might be getting messages from them or have them turning up at your door. Or you might be hearing from them through other concerned bystanders, sent in by the narcissist to play on your guilt, fear, obligation, and sympathy.

What you need right now is emotional safety. Talk to someone who understands the narcissist and won't place any blame on you. Tell yourself you are doing the right thing. And most importantly, do nothing to punish yourself. No bingeing on food, no ruminating or self-blame, no alcohol or drugs.

Practice **radical self-care**: treat yourself as you would a loved one who has suffered an injury. Here are some suggestions:

- Provide yourself with rest, good food, warm baths and even a bunch of flowers. Shop for and cook your favorite comfort food.
- Get some fresh air and gentle exercise.
- Listen to uplifting guided meditations on YouTube.
- Keep busy, put your house in order with some decluttering.
- Go for a swim or whatever exercise makes you feel good.
- Read a book or watch a funny movie.
- Make some plans for the future — a journey, a project, a new area of study.
- Get back in touch with nature: a walk in the forest or by the beach, or just a trip to your local park. Whatever it takes!

You can see from this list that it's about getting back to basics: doing the kinds of things that make a small child feel good. Keep it uncomplicated and know that you are doing the right thing by looking after yourself.

Switch your phone off if you need to and stay away from social media, where you may find your abuser trying to track you down. At this stage, you may be traumatized from the abusive contact and it's crucial to focus on calming yourself.

Stage 2: Moving forward and getting angry

Here, you'll start to feel your energy returning and you may have moments of rage and anger as you realize just how much time and energy the narcissist stole from you.

You might also feel angry at yourself — for letting the narcissist get away with their behavior for so long, for not speaking out or standing up for yourself. This is all totally normal and just means that you are moving forward and growing, not that you have failed or done anything wrong.

You may slip back into stage one, especially if you have contact with the narcissist. It's important at this stage to acknowledge your anger but not get stuck in it. Spending too much time online talking to other sufferers, for example, may not be the best idea as it can keep you from moving forward in your life.

If you find it really hard to move on, or you feel like you are going round in circles, this is a good time to see your GP and talk about getting some professional counseling, if you think it might help.

Stage Three: Should you get back in touch?

Now comes the point when you have forgotten some of the details of what went on, and more importantly, the unpleasant feelings may have faded. You start to remember the narcissist's good points. You begin to think that maybe it wasn't as bad as you remember, and maybe you were simply overreacting or being too sensitive.

Perhaps you want some closure, or a chance to see if they have mended their ways (they haven't.) Perhaps you simply miss the good times. You might also start to hear from the narcissist around now, as they begin to miss your attention and think of ways to lure you back in.

Remain strong. Don't go back — there is nothing there for you but pain. Letting the narcissist back into your world may send you straight back to stage one, or worse, you may find yourself back in a relationship with them, and the cycle begins again.

Stage Four: Achieving distance

This is the point at which you have had some time to heal and surround yourself with normalcy. You have moved past a lot of the fiercest emotions and you are starting to get a clearer understanding of what happened to you and why you were drawn into the relationship, or how you found your way out of it.

You may still have bad days, though, when you blame yourself or find yourself believing what the narcissist said about you.

Accept those feelings, sit with them, and they will pass. You are getting closer to being healed and moving forward with your life. The narcissist was wrong about you, and you did the best you could at the time.

Stage Five: Accepting and moving forward

You continue to move forward. You have a good understanding of your own strengths and weaknesses. Now, you are increasingly able to reject the things that the narcissist said to you.

Perhaps you have had some therapy and you are thinking about how to form healthier relationships in the future. You have formed some good daily habits to help you feel strong and safe (more on this later) and you are planning a happier life for yourself.

Above all, you are free of the narcissist and the toxic influence they held over your life.

5 Transformative Truths Every Victim Must Face

1.   The narcissist will never change in the way you need them to

Obviously, everyone is capable of change and personal growth. We all develop in all kinds of ways, some of us more than others. But the narcissist is very resistant to change, and you should never waste your time and energy hoping that things will be different.

For a start, it leaves you stuck in a position of waiting. And people can stay in that place for years. You may have moments when you see the possibility of things being different — for example, the narcissist has behaved badly, you have shut them out, and they are now luring you back in with promises that this time things will be different.

They won't. All that will happen, if you let that person get close again, is that the cycle will begin one more time. And then again and again. Even if they were to change, perhaps after many years of therapy, they will still be lacking in basic empathy. And do you really want to spend years of your one precious life waiting for someone to be better? All that time, all that energy, could be far more productively spent on other endeavors and more deserving people.

2. They aren't a different person with others and it wasn't you that was the problem.

Don't believe you are the only one to struggle with this person, although they may make you feel that way. Yes, it may seem like all is well in their other relationships, and you were the one that caused problems. But they aren't different towards other people. They are the same person with everyone.

The only difference is that you are seeing the outside of those other relationships, not the inside. Narcissists are incapable of treating anyone with kindness and decency. But they are also both secretive and obsessed with image, so chances are, their other relationships are also lacking and toxic, but they just hide it well.

3. They abused you deliberately and it wasn't "all in your head"

Because narcissists are so good at what they do, and at keeping their tricks just below the radar, you may start to wonder if you are imagining things. You might wonder if they are genuinely nasty and abusive, or if they somehow don't quite realize that what they are saying and doing is hurtful.

Yes. They know exactly what they are doing. There is no excuse for their behavior, although you will probably hear a few excuses: they are getting older (elderly narcissists are very good at hamming up their age when it suits them), or perhaps they had an unhappy childhood and you should actually feel sorry for them.

No. Sorry. Not good enough. Plenty of people have miserable childhoods and don't go around making others feel bad. There is no excuse for abusive behavior. This pity party is something that narcissists are very good at throwing when it suits them, particularly to target empathic individuals who will feel sorry for them and forgive them their behavior — only for it all to start up again one more time.

What compassionate people find hard to understand about narcissists is just how much pleasure they get from manipulating, exploiting and playing with others. Most of us don't enjoy those things and find it hard to imagine feeling happiness at the suffering of others. But narcissists do. They feed off the drama, the misery, and it gives them a sense of power, control and meaning in their otherwise empty lives. Sadly, there is no getting away from this, no higher self you can appeal to in the soul of a narcissist.

Nor is their abusive behavior accidental. A good question to ask yourself, if you are wondering about something a narcissist said or did, is — who was with you when they said that? Were you alone? Or did they say it in front of others? Anyone who can change how they behave depending on who is listening knows exactly what they are doing.

And even if they are unwell, it's not your problem. You have the right to protect yourself and live a life free of narcissistic abuse.

4.   Recovering will take time and isn't a process you can rush

Unlike a single traumatic event, such as a car crash, narcissistic abuse takes place over a long period of time. While physical wounds can heal, damage to your mental health takes longer.

What this means is that you don't have to forgive your abuser or sweep your feelings under the rug.

If you feel sad or angry about how you were treated, that isn't a sign of weakness. It's a reasonable response to what has happened to you. Nor do you need to forgive or feel compassion for your abuser. After all, they feel no compassion for you.

The narcissist wants you to doubt yourself, to minimize what happened and to believe that you are exaggerating or making it out to be worse than it was. This isn't true. Narcissists are truly dangerous and disruptive people, and you can take as long as you need to in healing from your experience.

5. All emotions are valid

There is no right way to feel. You may have felt, with your abuser, that certain feelings or reactions were unacceptable. Narcissistic parents are very good at training their children to subdue emotional responses and never complain, for example.

But all of your emotions are valid, and you have the right to feel them and express them appropriately, whatever they are. You have the right to feel **angry** for what has been said and done, as long as you aren't expressing your anger in a way that is destructive to others.

The trick is to use your anger productively: Use it to drive you forward, to energize you and to put your feelings into things that will further your own life. It can be a creative force for the good if you channel it and use it wisely!

You also have the right to feel **grief**. This isn't a weakness, it's an acknowledgment that you have lost someone you cared about, or at least the idea of who they were to you. Feel your grief, honour it, and move forward.

It can be helpful to take some distance from your emotions, to see them as separate to you: perhaps visualize your emotions as clouds that move through the sky. In the same way, they move through your body and simply pass. You don't need to fall apart: simply feel them, acknowledge what you are feeling, and let it sit with you for as long as you need to.

If you want to shift an unhelpful emotion, here are two things you can try.

- Bodywork: We hold emotions both good and bad in our body — just think of how differently we look, move and sound when we are feeling happy and when we are sad. So it makes sense, then, that bodywork is a way of shifting emotion. This might be through massage with a skilled therapist, yoga, meditation or a long walk. Swimming and being close to the water is also very healing for our emotions.

- Talking to a therapist skilled in post-traumatic stress disorder is also helpful as you work through emotions, and they will have specific techniques you can use to move forward.

Essential Exercises to Strengthen the Healing Heart & Mind

As you begin your healing journey, you may find journaling your thoughts and feelings useful. This can be a brain dump style of journaling, where you simply get all of your thoughts and memories out of your head and onto your page, or it can be a guided series of questions to help you ask yourself how you got into your relationship with the narcissist and what you have learned.

Narcissistic Relationship

Read on for some simple writing exercises that will clarify your inner thoughts and feelings and make moving forward a little easier by asking you some questions about your experience.

Find a time when you won't be interrupted and you are feeling strong, curious and ready to move forward in a significant way to get the most out of this exercise. Take as long as you need to, and feel free to return to these questions and your answers when you feel uncertain or upset. You will find your answers and your own inner wisdom very powerful. Ready? Let's go!

1. What are your false beliefs about the relationship?

Here, you can note down anything you believed about the person and your relationship with them that you now feel is false. Here are some ideas about things that you may have believed:

- Did you feel the problems were all your fault? None of us are perfect, but everything can't have been your fault. Start to unpick this and see if you gain a clearer picture of your relationship.
- Did you feel there were things you could have done to change the relationship?
- Did you feel he or she treated others better, or in fact does he or she treat everyone with a degree of contempt?
- Do you feel you will never find someone else? Is this true? Do you have other people in your life who care for you?

2. Is there anyone in your childhood who encouraged you to take on the blame?

- Sometimes, with a narcissist, we find ourselves taking on the blame for everything that has gone wrong, while the other person gets away looking like the innocent party.

- Is this a pattern from your childhood? Does it feel familiar to you? Is it true, or, like most children, were you just doing the best you could and making a few mistakes along the way?

3. What do you get out of protecting your abuser and taking the blame?

Perhaps you have some idealistic picture of how your relationship with this significant person should be, and you want to hold on to it. Perhaps you fear that if you stand up for youself you'll end up alone.

What is holding you back from facing up to the truth and leaving this person behind?

4. What are some alternative viewpoints you could come up with?

Finally, look at all the beliefs you have written down in part one, and come up with some alternatives that are realistic and feel true to you. For example, if you felt like it was all your fault, write down the ways in which you tried to make things better. Then list down the things that definitely weren't your fault and were simply the narcissist behaving badly.

Use this writing to return to when you are wavering or overcome with self-blame for what has unfolded. Taking the time to reflect on what has happened and challenging the status quo and the story your narcissist has told you is a way of replacing unhealthy beliefs with ones that are kinder and will help you move forward.

Life-Altering Affirmations to Heal Past Hurts

Add to your journal some affirmations that resonate with you, and use these to strengthen you when you are feeling overwhelmed. Again, this is something for your own private use and you can use it however you like, in ways that feel helpful and appropriate to you.

1. "I am healing."

This is perhaps the most powerful affirmation and one that you can use to counter any negative thought spirals when they come up. Healing is a long, slow process, but it can and does happen.

Healing may not be a straightforward or linear process, and there will be setbacks along the way. But you will heal.

2. "The past is behind me, and I am focusing on the present and the future."

It's easy, particularly when you are having a bad day, to get stuck in the past: regrets, rumination, thoughts about what you could have done differently or reliving horrible moments with the narcissist. Forgive yourself when this happens, and commit to the present and the future.

When you do get stuck in the past, the above affirmation can keep you steady. There is nothing any of us can do to change the past. All we can do is acknowledge what happened and use what it taught us to drive us into a happier future. It's also a good reminder to value the present moment.

3. "There is absolutely nothing wrong with this moment."

Again, the past can rear up to haunt us at vulnerable moments. When that happens, focus on the present. Stand outside, listen to the birds, feel the sun on your face and remind yourself that you are safe and free from harm.

Narcissistic Relationship

4. "I am a loveable person who deserves to be treated with respect and kindness."

This is the belief that narcissists are so very good at trying to dismantle. They are incapable of offering others love, respect, and kindness, or of feeling these things within themselves, so they do their best to make you feel like you don't deserve them, either.

Once you get away from a narcissist, you will need to work hardest at this affirmation. It means exactly what it says, and it is true!

5. "I deserve self-care."

This one is a life-long affirmation. We talked a little about self-care earlier in this chapter, and it is something that will really help you on your healing journey. It's also a way of putting yourself first — not all the time, of course, you're not a narcissist — but enough that you feel looked after and loved.

This isn't a selfish act; it's actually a way of ensuring you can take good care of others too. You can't fill up the tanks of others, such as your children and friends, when your own tank is running on empty. So look after yourself.

6. "I know what I know, and I trust myself."

Narcissists are experts at gaslighting and manipulating, making you doubt your own reality so they feel more powerful.
This affirmation seeks to counter that by putting you in charge of your own head and encouraging you to trust and believe your own intuition, thoughts, and feelings.

7. "I have the right to boundaries."

Protecting your boundaries is another act of self-care that you will need to work on as you recover from narcissistic abuse. It's particularly important as you can expect that the narcissist may lay low for a while, but will always return at some point to have another go at you.

Remain strong and unyielding, and quietly protect your boundaries at all times.

8. "They don't miss me; they miss the power."

If you feel sad for the narcissist because they seem lonely or try and get back in touch with you, remind yourself of who they really are with this affirmation. They never really loved you. It's not because of anything you did wrong, but because they simply aren't capable of love. What they do miss is having the power to mistreat you.

9. "My success is my response."

When anger strikes — and it will — don't lash out at them. This is exactly what they want you to do, as if you are showing emotion it means they still have power over you. Instead, repeat the above affirmation and use its energy to do something positive in your new life: work goals, a creative project, an exercise goal, or some self-care.

Work on things in your own life and let your happiness and future success be your revenge. Karma has a way of unfolding in its own sweet time — so you don't need to give it a push. You're too busy with other things.

10. "I have good friends and family around me."

As well as repeating this to yourself, seek out those who make you feel good and who you love and trust. Being around a narcissist is like

Narcissistic Relationship

being in a cold, dark room. Look for those people who make you feel like you're standing in a warm pool of sunlight, who treat you with kindness and warmth. Good friends and loving family members are the best antidotes to a narcissist you will ever meet. These can also include work colleagues, neighbors and the new people who appear unexpectedly when you make room for them — all those people in your life who treat you with respect and kindness. Treasure them, enjoy them and keep faith that they are out there.

Chapter 6 - Breaking the Cycle

In this chapter, we want to talk about how you can avoid narcissists in the future. We will look at why you might attract the attention of narcissists and how you can spot a narcissist

Finally, we'll get creative and provide you with some methods for developing self-love and self-care, along with various practices to cultivate inner peace and happiness. These techniques will not only make you feel good, they will also provide you with protection against any narcissists in your life. Let's get started.

6 Reasons Why You Keep Attracting Narcissists

First of all, I need to clarify the above statement. It's estimated that around 6% of the population suffers from Narcissistic Personality Disorder. So if you are out and about a lot, working, going out and meeting people in your daily life, chances are you will come across a narcissist or two.

The trouble isn't encountering them or even attracting them. Because they burn through relationships more than most people, they also tend to hone in on anyone new, seeking fresh attention. The problem is letting them hang around. Narcissists are very good at spotting those who are going to put up with them, and who are therefore ripe to be exploited. So it's not about attracting narcissists — we all do at times — it's about letting them in your door.

Here are some questions to ask yourself about why you may have accepted a narcissist into your life that will help you both understand yourself better and be more aware in future about what to look for at the start of a relationship.

1. Do you tend to put up with other people's selfishness?

Some of us are more tolerant than others, and if you suffer from low self-esteem or were raised in an environment where you were expected to accommodate selfish behavior, such as that of a parent, you may be conditioned to put up with selfishness. Narcissists will very quickly work out who will put up with their games and who won't and will hone in on those who tend to be more accepting and easy-going.

You don't need to be too wary or suspicious — after all, most people aren't narcissists. But don't feel you have to let everyone in straight away. Taking the time to get to know people slowly is a better strategy and if you do notice someone seems a little selfish — dominating in conversation, letting you pay for everything — take note and slow down in what you give them.

2. Do you have boundaries around what you will and won't tolerate from others?

This can apply to friends, family and romantic partners equally. If you are someone who tends to feel taken advantage of, you may also be a target for narcissists. Look first at your own treatment of others — are you respectful of others, do you ensure you treat everyone as you would like to be treated yourself? Once you know you respect other's boundaries, why not insist that your boundaries are also protected?

This means thinking about how you would like others to treat you, and speaking up when you aren't happy about something. It's something you can learn to do, so if you feel like this may be one of the things that the narcissist saw in you, look into ways of strengthening your boundaries — we will cover some here, but a few sessions with a therapist is a great starting point.

3. Do you tend to stay for longer than you should in a bad relationship?

Backing out of a relationship that started off well but has since gone downhill is not always easy to do. At what point do you end it? How do you go about it? Should you stay, just to see if it improves?

If you are someone who finds it hard to know when to finish something, when to let go and move on, you may sadly be someone that narcissists are drawn to. If you feel that a relationship hasn't turned out as you would like, and you are unsure about whether you should leave or stay, there are a few things you can do.

First of all, remember that relationships are always changing. They get better or worse, but they never stay the same. The trick is to look at the pattern — if the relationship started off well but has steadily worsened, and you are feeling bad about yourself, then it's time to step away. It's simply not worth your precious time and energy to stay in a relationship that isn't making you happy. Never.

4. Are you someone who puts up with being devalued?

A narcissist will always start out lovely and charming, but let them in, and you'll start to see their true self. This may start with a subtle put-down or slightly off comment. Or you may realize that they never have their wallet during dates. Overall, they seem to always take more than they give in terms of time, energy, and effort.

If you are someone who has a tendency to put up and shut up, you are the ideal target for a narcissist. This doesn't mean that you have to get into a shouting match with them when they behave badly, it just means that you need to watch out for this tendency to be too much of a people-pleaser. Ensure that the people you bestow your time and kindness upon truly deserve it, and give it back, too.

5. Do you tend to excuse other people's bad behavior?

It's good to give people the benefit of the doubt. Everyone has bad days and no one is perfect. But if someone's behavior is consistently difficult and you find you are always trying to find an excuse for it, this is a big warning sign.

6. If someone is abusive, do you leave immediately?

This, more than anything, is a huge red flag. We all have different levels of what we will tolerate, depending on how we were raised and our own temperament and personality. If someone grew up with a parent who was violent, for example, they might have been groomed to see this behavior as acceptable or simply what happens in relationships.

If you feel you are someone who puts up with more than you should, get curious about this. Talk to a therapist or do some reading about what constitutes emotional abuse as well as physical abuse. Learn more about listening to your gut instinct and the warning signs of abuse. All of these things can be learned and will protect you from harm in the future.

7 Ways to Spot a Narcissist on the First Date

As we now know, narcissists are good at charming others, at seeming incredibly caring and understanding — until you get to know them. Then, it's a different story. But how do you filter them out before you get hurt? It's not easy, feeling a connection with someone makes it even harder. Fortunately, there are some warning signs.

1. They have planned out the date out in detail

People who can't plan anything can be frustrating and at first sight, someone who seems to be in control of every detail of a first date may be a welcome change.

But pay attention to those early interactions — do they let you choose the venue, or do they insist on deciding? When you get there, do they say "Would you like me to order?" or do you make that decision together?

Someone who seems to want to be in control of every detail may be simply organized, or they might have a controlling and narcissistic personality. It's too early to tell either way — but just be curious, and take note.

2. Love bombing

We've already looked at this in detail, but it's worth mentioning again as it's such a typical narcissistic trait, and one that can easily win you over if you aren't clued into it. If your date agrees with absolutely everything you say, something is up. No one is that nice or that agreeable. While it's flattering to have someone so seemingly in tune with you, if you start to feel like you're being played, you probably are.

Also look out for dates who start making too many plans, too quickly. On a first date, you should feel like you have a little time to breathe and reflect afterward, not find yourself lining up another meeting straight away.

Narcissists are very good at charming people and then before you know it they are in your life, settling in and taking over your time, your energy and your money. Be cautious. If something seems too good to be true, it usually is.

3. Lots of subtle bragging

It's an interesting fact that those who genuinely have the most to brag out — wealth, success, talent, beauty — tend not to brag at all. Instead, they seek to make others feel good because they have no need to seek approval from others themselves.

The out-and-out braggers are easy to spot and almost comical in their efforts to boast and impress with their money, power and success. But watch out, too, for the humblebraggers and the stealthy boasts that gradually add up to a picture of someone who feels that they're superior to everyone else. These are the really skilled narcissists, and if you noticed a few too many brags, you may be in the company of one.

4. They are rude to staff

How someone treats wait staff and others who are there to serve is always telling. Do they demand, complain and act superior, or do they make jokes on their behalf or try to humiliate them? Do they insist on sitting in a particular spot, or have some kind of problem with the restaurant's environment? If you see someone doing these things, it's a big warning sign that they may soon treat you the same way.

Being rude or getting angry over everyday annoyances like slow service in a restaurant is also a sign that they may have problems with anger management. Sure, everyone has bad days and gets annoyed, but if someone seems to have no sense of perspective and can't keep their cool in public, you may have a problem.

And also look out for anything weird around money — as we have discovered, narcissists tend to be bad gift-givers and are often stingy with money. Red flags here include suddenly disappearing to the restroom when it's time to pay the bill, refusing to leave a tip, or forgetting their wallet.

5. What they say they want and their history don't add up

If someone acts like they are desperate to settle down, marry and have children, be cautious. No one should be talking long-term on a first date (or second, third, or fourth...) Dig a little deeper and ask about someone's recent romantic history. Do they have a series of short-term relationships and dramatic breakups behind them? Do they have ex-partners that they still talk about a lot? All of these points may mean that you are in the company of a narcissist who tends to churn and burn through romantic partners.

6. They get you to reveal your insecurities but guard their own

Narcissists are very good at probing and digging around to find your weaknesses and the things you feel a little sensitive about. In time, they will use these to make themselves feel more superior and to needle you when they want to put you in your place.

Yet, you will never see them admitting their own insecurities in any meaningful way. While you spill your secrets, they will simply listen, smile and perhaps say something cutting to twist the knife a little.

If you come away from a date feeling like you've been way too candid and vulnerable, it may be a sign that you've just met a narcissist. Meeting new people should make you feel good, uplifted, encouraged — it shouldn't make you feel small or exposed.

7.   It's all about them

The best conversations are a two-way street — some listening, some talking, some shared laughs, and observations. But not so with the narcissist, who isn't there to learn, listen and enjoy, but to be admired and fawned over. If someone talks non-stop, and you find yourself needing to disappear to the restroom just to get a break from their incessant chatter, be warned — this is your future.

If every anecdote you tell seems to segue into a similar story about something they did, but better, it's yet another warning bell. Narcissists find it very hard to listen. Usually, they seem distracted, they fiddle with their phone or don't quite meet your eye. They prefer to be discussing their own skills and talents than learning more about the people around them. If it's all about them, prepare yourself for the possibility that you may be in the company of a narcissist.

Another thing you might notice is that they talk very flatteringly of other people they know — friends, work colleagues, family members. You feel yourself getting ever-smaller in comparison to these wonderful people, and wonder why you are spending a date hearing about how special someone else was — shouldn't there be some focus on you? (Answer: yes.)

What to do if you realize all this on the first date?

Don't panic. Enjoy the evening for what it is (a learning experience!) and be sure to debrief with a trusted friend afterward. Spotting a narcissist early and setting up your boundaries accordingly is a useful life skill and one that is worth knowing!

4 Ways to Stop Attracting Narcissists Once and for All

If you feel like you keep attracting this type of person into your life, you are probably desperate to halt the pattern. After all, why would anyone want to invite such difficult people into their lives?

The truth is, the narcissist is there to teach you something. And until you learn it, they will keep coming back. See them as a teaching tool and they are suddenly so much easier to deal with. But what are they there to teach?

Essentially, it's people-pleasers that seem to attract narcissists. Docile, easy-going types are their favored prey. If this is you, there are ways you can change this dynamic.

1.   Don't make so many excuses for people

If someone behaves badly, they are in the wrong. Full stop. It doesn't matter how hard their childhood was, how stressful their job is — there is no excuse for abusive behavior. Don't excuse it. Don't empathize. You aren't their doctor and you aren't their punching bag. It's not your problem and you can't fix anyone but yourself.

Yes, it's hard to walk away from people. It's hard to accept that you can't fix someone, even if you care for them. It's hard when you know how forgiving you are, how kind and how good the relationship would be, if only they weren't so nasty. But you need to put yourself and your own physical and emotional safety first.

If someone is abusive towards you, walk away. It truly is the key to a happy and safe life, and you deserve it.

2.   Spot the red flags and trust your instincts

We have covered red flags in detail, and you are now well-armed with a checklist of signs to look out for.

Take note of them, trust your instincts, and if you feel like you aren't safe, back away. Resist the urge to stay in a situation that makes you uneasy because you don't want to be rude or cause trouble.

You don't have to tell the person why you are no longer available — in fact, with a narcissist, it's better that you don't, as they love confrontation and showdowns. Simply back away, disengage and make it clear that your time and energy are being taken up elsewhere.

3.   Don't let yourself get overpowered

Something narcissists are very good at is wearing down their victims. This may be with long, exhausting conversations where you literally cannot escape. It may be by waking you up early or keeping you up late at night so you feel tired and less able to make clear decisions. It may be by keeping you under close scrutiny — watching what you do, asking lots of questions and making lots of comments so you feel self-conscious and targetted.

Be aware of this tendency, and if you feel yourself getting swamped, find a way to free yourself. Get off the phone, go to bed early, go home. Take some time and space to re-energize — a swim, a workout, some meditation or a long walk — and then deal with them. If a narcissist knows that you have clear boundaries around your time and energy, they will move on to someone else.

If it's a good, healthy relationship, they won't mind you taking things slowly.

4.   Seek help from a skilled therapist

If you find yourself involved in these relationships again and again, it may be that you need to unpick the deeper reasons with the help of a skilled therapist. This will take time and money, but it may be the best investment you ever make in yourself and your future.

9 Powerful Tips for Developing Unbreakable Self-Love

A tried-and-tested way to protect yourself from narcissists is to develop self-love. This isn't about being egotistical or narcissistic yourself; it's about looking after yourself in the same way you would a good friend or a small child. Here, I've gathered together some simple techniques and ideas to really work on your self-love.

This is something that a narcissist cannot take away from you, and that will keep you safe in the future.

1.   Start each day by setting mindful intentions

Intention setting is essentially telling yourself you are worthy of care and love. Start each day with a few moments of mindful breathing and set your intention for the day, which may be something as simple as "Today I am going to take care of myself and show myself love in everything I do because I deserve it."

It may sound strange, but say this — or create a personal message or mantra that works for you — and you will see the benefits. Essentially, a loving mantra or intention sends a signal to your subconscious that you are worthy of love and care that slowly but surely challenges all those negative messages that were given to you by the narcissist.

2.   Treat yourself as a friend or small child

If you are feeling down about yourself and can't seem to shake off feelings of low self-esteem, think of yourself as someone else — perhaps a good friend or a small child. What would you do to make him or her feel better? What would you advise? If you were a wise and compassionate friend, what would you tell yourself to feel better? If you were looking after a small child, would you feed her a good meal, run her a warm bath and give her a comforting story in bed?

Writing a letter to yourself is another powerful way to tap into your inner wisdom and kindness. Write down everything you would say to yourself and when you read it back later, you'll be amazed at how powerful your words can be. Keep your letters and read them back to yourself when you need clarity or a bit of support.

3. Acknowledge your feelings

Somethings, simply naming your feelings — *I feel sad*, or *I feel regret* — can be a way of moving through them. We are very good at escaping our feelings in all sorts of ways: numbing out on social media, alcohol, shopping, overeating.

But sometimes taking the time to really feel them — sitting with them, going for a long walk or swim, or writing them down — is the best way to integrate and learn. Instead of always trying to escape, befriend your feelings and you will soon find that they are simply feelings, not a concrete, fixed reality, and they will pass.

4. Treat yourself in healthy ways

Life is here to be enjoyed and savored. If you have found yourself in a relationship with a narcissist, you may have forgotten this. You may be feeling worn out, discouraged and small.

Take back control and treat yourself with acts of kindness and positivity, as you would someone who is recovering from an illness or accident. What are your favorite ways to relax — a funny movie, a holiday, your favorite home-cooked meal in front of the TV, a hot bath or a long swim or walk in the forest?

Make a priority of yourself for a change — do all those things that make you feel good, and leave time to do them regularly.

5.   Meditate

The benefits of meditation are now well known, and regular meditation is a surefire way to boost feelings of calm, happiness and control. Thanks to the internet, it's easy to meditate — just search for guided meditations online, find a quiet space to sit or lie down, and give yourself ten minutes or longer to meditate — you'll soon notice the benefits of increased clarity and joy.

6.   Feel gratitude

It's easy to get ground down by everything that goes wrong, particularly if you have a narcissist in your life reminding you of your every flaw and failure. But research consistently shows that it's feelings of gratitude, not money, wealth or success, that lead to good self-worth.

Take a moment when you remember to think of everything in your life that you feel grateful for — your friends, your health, everything that went well that day, from a small conversation to a quiet moment to reading a good book. Feeling gratitude for the small pleasures of life is the true key to happiness.

7.   Look after your body

While focusing on meditation and healthy self-talk will take care of your mind, don't forget about your body. Eating well, drinking lots of water, getting enough sleep and getting some regular exercise — even if it's just a gentle walk or a ten-minute workout video or dancing around the house — are all essential for happiness.

It's so easy nowadays to live in our heads — online or lost in thoughts — while our bodies are neglected. But if you are coming out of a bad relationship, taking care of your physical self is just as important as your emotional wellbeing. And if fact, when your head is a mess, it's sometimes a good idea to go back to basics — food, water, exercise, sleep — as a way of rebuilding your wellbeing.

8. Give back

What selfish people don't realize is that giving to others can reward the giver just as much as the recipient. Taking the time to offer kindness to others is a way of taking care of yourself — volunteer, spend some time playing with a child, raise some money for a good cause, or help a friend out. You'll feel your own happiness rise along with those you are helping.

9. Plan for the future

Once you have taken care of the present moment, spend some time making your future brighter. What can you do today that will make you feel better in a year's time? Think of what you would like to do and where you would like to be and reverse-engineer the process by thinking of what you can do now to get there.

Maybe you need to do some further training or look for some freelance work to fund a dream holiday. Maybe you want to be healthier and fitter, so today you need to push yourself to go for a run. Maybe you want to write a book, so today you set aside an hour to write 500 words.

Keeping a big picture to-do list of what you want your life to look like will guide you in your daily choices and keep you focused on your happiness and life goals.

Chapter 7 - Loving Again

So you've begun to recover from your relationship with a narcissist and you're ready to move forward. Or are you? In this chapter, we'll look at dating and how you can avoid making the same mistakes again with your new partner.

We'll also cover some attitude shifts you need to make so you can enjoy better relationships. We've covered red flags to look out for, and in this chapter, we'll go one step further and look at the early signs that show you've found a good partner. Finally, we'll cover good habits to get a new relationship off to a healthy start.

You can set the terms of a relationship to some extent, and the start is the best time to do it. Ideally, you will have spent some time thinking about relationships and your own patterns, and you will be feeling fresh and energized and ready to venture out into the world of dating again.

What can you do to ensure that your new relationships get off to the very best start? Plenty, as it happens. But first of all, let's look at some things you should definitely avoid.

7 Mistakes to Avoid When You Start Dating Again

If you have been in a relationship with a narcissist, you may still be carrying unhelpful beliefs about what a partner should say and do. Your judgment can be skewed by spending time with the wrong people. You may also feel as if your confidence has taken a hit. First of all, there's no need to rush straight back out into dating.

Give yourself as much time as you need to recover, using any or all of the ideas I mentioned in the previous chapter. Always bear in mind that you'll need to tread carefully to avoid making the same mistakes again.

Here are some common pitfalls to look out for when you start dating again.

1.   **Hiding the truth of who you are**

In the the world of dating, it can feel that we need to present ourselves as a shiny package, with interesting hobbies, a great body, and a happy, untroubled face. Don't fall into that trap. Be honest about who you are with everyone you meet, don't feel you have to please or impress, and you will find that the right people come to you.

What if you read this and think — but I don't know who I am? Get curious. Get to know and feel comfortable with yourself, either on your own or with the guidance of a therapist, so when you step out into the world you'll feel more certain of what you're about and less likely to be unsettled by a narcissist.

2.   **Rushing in too quickly**

As we've seen already, narcissists are adept at moving fast at the start of a new relationship, only for it to fall apart fairly quickly once the initial buzz wears off. Be aware of this tendency when you meet someone and look out for love bombing. Most importantly, take it slow. Don't get drunk and go home with your date that first night, and definitely don't share all your secrets.

Take any outrageous love bombing or commitment talk with a large pinch of salt. If it's meant to be, taking your time won't make a difference. On this note, and it has to be said, don't sleep with someone on the first date if you are thinking it might be a longer-term relationship.

3. Expecting them to commit exclusively

As above, take things slowly. Dating is all about getting to know people, and you can't expect someone to commit just to you on a first date, or even second or third. If someone seems ready to sweep you away and is already talking about an exclusive relationship after three hours in your company, don't fall for it! Someone who falls into infatuation this fast is likely to fall out of it just as quickly, and you are the one who will get burned.

4. Forgetting to enjoy yourself

It's easy to feel like it's all destined to fail after a bad relationship. If you are feeling cynical and bitter, it might be that you're not yet ready or you just haven't found the right person.

You had a bad experience, and that can put you off the whole world of dating in the same way that a bout of food poisoning can put your off the particular food for life. But remember, dating can also be fun. There are — believe it or not — lots of decent, kind, caring people out there who just want to meet someone themselves to spend time with.

You had some bad luck. But it's not your destiny. With some self-care and time to reflect, you will have done some important personal growth that will stand you in good stead when you are ready to try again. Try not to take it too seriously and remember the benefits of mindfulness and gratitude as you move forward. Life is there to be enjoyed, otherwise, what's the point?

An important disclaimer: if you really aren't enjoying life or you feel genuinely anxious and depressed, all the uplifting messages, mindfulness and gratitude in the world might not be enough to make you feel better. Always, always reach out and seek help if you are struggling. See your GP, talk to someone.

5.   Seeing a partner as the be-all and end all

You can be perfectly happy single. Oddly, for many people, it's only when they are truly happy on their own and not looking to meet anyone that they actually find someone to commit to.

If you feel that finding someone is an urgent priority in your life, you need to step back a little. Find ways of enjoying time on your own. Spend a whole day on your own doing things you enjoy, make friends with yourself and give yourself the kind of company you would enjoy from someone else.

If you really do feel that finding someone is a matter of urgency, you will only make things harder for yourself. New relationships thrive best in an atmosphere of ease and unhurried fun.

6.   Not keeping an open mind

If you have an idea of what your new partner should be like and it's absolutely set in stone, you're going to run into problems. That ideal partner might not exist. Or the ideal partner for you might be nothing like the one you have in your head. My advice is to keep an open mind in general, not just with dating. Be flexible and try new experiences (while always maintaining safe boundaries and looking after yourself).

7.   Not trusting your gut

This is probably the most important thing you can do to avoid repeating the same mistake with a relationship. Sure, you might really like someone. They might be attractive, funny, charming and seem to be really into you. It all looks wonderful on the surface as they say and do all the right things.

But how does it feel?

As humans, we are wired to pick up on all sorts of non-verbal signals when interacting with others to work out if they are safe or not. We aren't aware of them a lot of the time, so we can get into the habit of overriding or ignoring these messages from our unconscious if they don't fit in with what we think we want — a relationship, someone to go out with, marriage, babies...
But listening to, and trusting your gut — and then responding to what it is telling you — is one of the smartest things you can do for both your physical and emotional safety.

It may mean being rude and leaving a date or not going home with someone who is incredibly charming and persuasive. It may mean getting told you're rude or difficult.

Don't worry. If you are with someone, and your gut feels tense, or you feel a general sense of uneasiness that you can't quite shake off, believe those messages, and get away as quickly as you can.

If there is one message I hope you will take away from this book, it's this: ***Always trust your gut.***

5 Early Signs You've Finally Found a Good Partner

Now that we've discovered what not to do when we start dating again, let's move onto the good stuff: finding someone who is going to make your world a happier place, not turn it upside down. There are many signs you can look out for that will show you you're on the right track with a new partner.

Here are some things to look out for when you start dating that will signal you've found someone you are compatible with.

1.   You feel physically at ease in their presence

If you're with someone who is good for you, who isn't going to harm you, you will probably get a warm and easy feeling. The conversation will flow smoothly most of the time. You won't find yourself worrying about what you've said or done, and you will be enjoying yourself.

You'll feel physically safe, comfortable and relaxed. Look for those feelings when you start dating and believe in them, even if the person isn't necessarily your dream partner in every way — sometimes it happens that way.

2.   You share common interests and concerns

No matter how attractive someone is or how charming, in a long-term relationship, there needs to be more than just chemistry. If you feel that you share some similar interests and passions, it's a great sign of compatibility. This does not mean someone who agrees with everything you say. It's more about sounding out your world view and knowing pretty quickly that the other person in on the same page.

This isn't to say that you need to be compatible in all ways. In fact, it's great to have some areas where you have absolutely nothing in common. Someone with different interests can teach you about things you've never found interesting before. On the other hand, having interests that your partner doesn't share gives you a sense of space and allows you to maintain a separate identity.

Keep in mind that it's good to enjoy time off in the same way. If you love traveling and your prospective partner does not own a passport, a lifelong relationship may not be in the cards. If they are hugely invested in a hobby — cycling, gaming, running — that doesn't interest you at all, you might need to manage your expectations about their availability.

But if you find that you enjoy at least some of the same things — even if it's as simple as cuddling up on the couch together watching old movies — then chances are you'll enjoy each other's company.

3. They turn up when they say they will

Narcissists are great at running late, creating drama with last-minute cancellations and let-downs. They make a great deal of fuss around the simple act of gracing you with their presence. It's not surprising that being around them can feel hectic and stressful.

What does the opposite experience look like? If someone just shows up on time, looking friendly and relaxed, and you have a nice time together — talking, chatting, walking, seeing a movie or just enjoying a coffee together — you can start to let down your guard and relax.

When you start seeing someone, it should feel like getting to know a friend or work colleague more than a scene straight out of a Hollywood movie. It should feel relaxed, easy, fun. You should feel curious and enlivened, not overwhelmed or swamped with emotion and chemistry. There should be some chemistry, yes, but it shouldn't feel too urgent or over-the-top.

4. They are consistently kind and interested in you

Remember when we looked at intermittent reinforcement? The opposite of this is consistency. If someone is nice to you, but only sometimes, my advice would be to back off. But if someone is consistently pleasant and kind — not over the top, just decent — then you may well be in the presence of a keeper.

Don't waste your time on someone who is only available sometimes, or who gives you just the crumbs of their attention. Generally, if someone likes you, **you know it**. It's not a mystery. If you find yourself wondering about where you stand with someone, it's likely that you aren't their top priority.

5. You share similar lifestyles

Sleep, food, exercise, levels of tidiness and daily habits such as reading or exercising — all of these mundane things make up the way you live your life. If you see some compatibility in the small things, then that is a very good sign for your future together. If you walk into someone's house and like the way it looks and feels (rather than feeling impressed, awed, or just slightly nonplussed), you should trust that feeling. A long-term relationship isn't about mindblowing passion and chemistry. It's about enjoying your daily life together, and your daily habits are a big part of this.

On this note, if you want to make your life easier, pay attention to how someone presents themselves and their living space. If they appear uncared for or chaotic, that should give you pause. And if that person is dependent on alcohol or other substances, be aware that they may not have the resources to be a good partner.

8 Great Habits to Start Your New Relationship the Right Way

1.   Slow and steady

Hold back when you meet someone new. Remember, if they are the one you have all the time in the world to enjoy that fact. If they are not, you should enjoy the relationship for what it is, but also protect yourself so you don't find yourself having to heal and recover from a disastrous relationship.

2.   Treat them as you would like to be treated

Set the tone for the relationship you would like to have with someone by being that person yourself. Be kind. Be on time. Communicate as clearly as you can. A new relationship is a fresh start, and you can steer it in the right direction by being respectful and positive.

Even when arguments come along — and they will — remember that you have something special between you and you need to look after that, even if you are having a temporary disagreement. It's possible to fight with someone while still remaining respectful and not doing any permanent damage to the bond between you.

If it's meant to be, you'll have set the groundwork for a rich and loving relationship by treating your partner as you would like to be treated.

3.   Focus on the other person

To build a strong relationship takes time and effort. It's often the result of many daily interactions, and learning to focus on someone and respond to them is a useful skill for any relationship, not just a romantic one.

To do this, first of all, eliminate distractions. Make time to spend with your partner, switch off screens, listen and focus. Even if you are busy and rushing off in separate directions, eye contact and affection can go a long way in maintaining a healthy and loving connection into the future.

4. Look after yourself

Just because you've met someone new, this doesn't give you an excuse to stop your efforts to heal from your experience with a narcissist. Keep doing all those things you did to recover — talking to a therapist, looking after your physical and mental wellbeing, journaling and spending time alone to rest and recharge. Taking time out to reflect on where the relationship is going and how you are feeling is another way of looking after yourself as you move forward.

Even in the early days, get in the habit of setting aside some personal space, even if you feel like being with them all the time. Give them time to miss you and feel curious about what you've been up to. It's important to give yourself time to enjoy your own company.

5. Don't dwell in the past

Whatever happened with the narcissist, don't let yourself dwell too much on it if it makes you feel bad. Of course, you need to spend some time on it, either alone or with a therapist, but don't live there. When you find yourself ruminating or wondering how the narcissist is going, bring yourself firmly back into the present with self-care or distraction.

On this note, don't assume that all of your future partners are going to let you down. If you have done some work on yourself and reflected on what may have led you to your narcissistic partner, you should be able to avoid carrying this baggage into your new relationship. Give this new person a chance.

6. Remind yourself of how far you have come

If you have been in a relationship with a narcissist, you've been through quite an experience. Always remind yourself of the fact that you got yourself away, you are now safe, and you have a lot to look forward to.

If you find yourself regretting the time you spent with them, remind yourself that you have a whole future ahead of you that they no longer have the power to ruin. You are safe. You deserve to be happy.

7. Don't badmouth the relationship to others

If you are starting out with someone, it's sometimes a good idea to let it grow in its own time, and in private, before you start talking about it too much to others. It's natural to want to share your new relationship with friends, but just be mindful of how much you share. Try to keep some things private. There are a couple of reasons for this.

First, letting others into your new world with this person too quickly, particularly if they prefer you single, can have a negative impact on the new relationship. Secondly, talking about the relationship in detail with others has a way of taking away energy from its growth and opening up the new bond you have formed to the influence of others, who may not have your best interests at heart.

If you aren't sure about how it's going but generally feel OK, talk to your new partner, or your journal, or your therapist. And if you feel suddenly upset, don't go rushing off to badmouth your new partner to your friends. A new relationship is a fragile thing, like a seedling or tiny baby, and you need to treat it will care as it grows stronger.

8. Laugh together

Sharing humor is one of the best ways to relieve stress and bond with your partner. And it's what makes being in a relationship with someone so much fun. So don't forget to laugh, enjoy each other's company, and be silly together.

A final word on finding new love

As you move on from the narcissist, remember to be positive and hopeful for the future, but also realistic. Unfortunately, there are some people out there you need to steer well clear of for your own wellbeing and happiness. But there are also many others who will enrich your life. Ultimately, it's about finding that sweet spot between keeping yourself safe and trusting in those that you meet to do the right thing by you.

If the relationship you've had with a narcissist is good for anything, it's that you have learned how to look after yourself in all sorts of new ways. Believe in your new insights, get out there, and have fun!

Narcissistic Relationship

Conclusion

Hopefully, in this book, you've found out more about yourself and other people. Use this knowledge to enjoy healthy, satisfying, and joyful relationships. We've been on a journey together, and my sincere wish is that you are feeling energized, educated, and ready to face the future.

Let's take a moment to go over the key points of this book.

First, we looked at the reasons for picking it up in the first place: you suspect you may be in a relationship with a narcissist, and you want to find out more. Or you've come out of a bad relationship and you are now wondering — what happened? You may also want to avoid making the same mistakes again or prevent others from doing so.

I firmly believe that you should know your enemy. And getting to know the narcissist and what makes him or her tick is a tool that will stand you in good stead as you move through life.

We also looked at the key traits of narcissists that make them so easy to spot: primarily, a grandiose sense of self, an unshakeable belief that they are special and uniquely talented. They also have a shameless ability to exploit people, abuse others, and put themselves first.

We also looked at what makes someone a narcissist and how a childhood that combines excessive spoiling with periods of neglect is often what sows the seeds of a narcissistic personality disorder. We saw that despite the strong and overpowering way they present themselves, it's actually very lonely inside the narcissist's head, and they aren't nearly as powerful as they need you to think they are.

Narcissistic Relationship

We discovered the key warning signs of narcissists, and some of their most common tactics, including gaslighting, love bombing, intermittent reinforcement, and narcissistic rage. The manipulative tactics of narcissists can be quite unsettling to those who are used to more straightforward communication, but once you know and understand them, you are better equipped to deal with them. And most importantly, you've stopped wondering if it's all in your head.

You now know many of the telling phrases that narcissists come out with and what triggers them. You can identify the kinds of people they are attracted to — usually kind and empathic souls who tend to give others the benefit of the doubt. We also looked at how to avoid triggering the narcissist and feeling the full fury of one of their attacks.

Simply put, you can't reason with a narcissist and you can't expect the same reasonable responses from them that you would get from others. Being around a narcissist is not like being around most people — what you need to focus on is primarily protecting yourself, and also managing them so that they can keep themselves under control.

An important point we touched on here is that the narcissist can't change. There is nothing you can do that will improve their behavior, and accepting this and moving forward as best you can is the only sane response.

We then moved on to how this affects their victims. We looked at the damage it can do to you, and why you must leave or disengage for your own wellbeing. Narcissists are very good at manipulating their victims, at holding on tightly when they show signs of leaving and at making a clean break as difficult as possible.

But once you are aware of this, and can keep in mind your own future mental health and wellbeing, you will find within yourself the power to cut the cord for good. The sad thing here is accepting that the narcissist isn't really capable of love or caring relationships, and you need to give up on the hope that you will ever receive what you need from them.

The second part of the book was more active and required more input from you, with lots of techniques and strategies to move forward in your new life, free from this troubling personality.

We looked at how to leave, and the Gray Rock Method as a way of making the narcissist lose interest in you.

We then looked at healing — how to get yourself back to neutral after this disturbing experience, and from there, how to re-energize yourself and move forward with courage, strong self-esteem, and hope.

You discovered all kinds of ways to make yourself stronger and healthier, so that the narcissist can't find a way back in. Mental health options include therapy, meditation, self-love, mantras, and journaling. You can strengthen yourself physically with food, sleep, and exercise. There are so many ways to heal yourself, and I hope you find ones that work for you and enjoy the numerous benefits.

Finally, we looked at breaking the cycle so you don't find yourself in this situation again. We covered what to look for in a relationship, early warning signs, and the signals that you are on the right track to a healthier and more satisfying future.

You deserve to be treated well, you deserve a loving relationship, and I honestly believe that if you do the growth work and take care of yourself, you can find it. Sometimes, a book isn't enough and you need some real-life guidance too: I hope you have the resources and courage to explore further with a trained and compatible therapist, should you need to.

I hope you have enjoyed the journey and found it useful. Narcissists are incredibly frustrating to deal with, and they can do a lot of damage. I wish it weren't the case, but chances are, even if you never have a close relationship with one, you will come across them in your life, your work and your day to day dealings with the world.

Sometimes, you can't simply ignore them. They are widely acknowledged by psychologists as some of the hardest people to treat, so taking the time to read up on them and learn more is a good use of your time and energy. Human nature is fascinating, and you may even get to the point where you can simply enjoy the quirks of a narcissist in your family or working life without being too affected by them.

You now have a whole bunch of effective strategies to deal with narcissists that you can put in place and use as often as you need to (hopefully not at all, but you can't guarantee that!) You know how to look after yourself, how to back away, and how to form healthier and more satisfying relationships with those that will appreciate your presence, time and energy. You know that even if narcissists make it hard for you to leave, you still have the right to do so.

If there is one thing I would like you to take away from this book, it's to **trust your instincts and do whatever you need to to keep safe and happy**. There is no need to suffer with those who aren't good for you, and to give them your time and energy that could be better spent elsewhere.

Narcissists truly are vampires that walk among us, feeding on the good energy of others and at ease with exploiting your kindness and generosity. Don't feel bad about moving away from them, however much they cry and wail. Say no, protect your boundaries, put yourself and your own wellbeing first. You deserve so much more than that from your relationships — and you can have it.

www.ingramcontent.com/pod-product-compliance
Lightning Source LLC
Chambersburg PA
CBHW031110080526
44587CB00011B/907